WORKBOOK for C

Yedidyah Langsam

Brooklyn College of C.U.N.Y.

SIMON & SCHUSTER CUSTOM PUBLISHING

Printed in the United States of America

10 9 8 7 6 5 4 3 2 1

ISBN 0-536-59699-9
BA 96227

SIMON & SCHUSTER CUSTOM PUBLISHING
160 Gould Street/Needham Heights, MA 02194
Simon & Schuster Education Group

CONTENTS

TO THE STUDENT

To learn to write computer programs, you must learn to devise algorithms— plans of attack— to solve the problems that you will be given. After that, you must write the program precisely to carry out your plan. Planning the program is the most important part of the programming process. First, plan your algorithm carefully. Ask yourself what techniques you have learned which pertain to this problem. Ask yourself how you would do this problem without a computer. Break the problem into smaller parts, if possible, and plan the large picture first, leaving the details for later consideration. Working problems in this book will give you practice in using the techniques of the C language. That practice will help you when you are planning algorithms, and it will help you write programs more effectively. With sufficient practice, you will know which technique to use to solve a particular problem. Repeated practice with the problems will lessen chances for errors in the programs you submit, and save you time in correction and resubmission. (No one can write error-free programs the first time every time, however.) The problems in this book will also prepare you for similar problems on examinations. In fact, many of the problems presented here have been taken from old examinations.

ORGANIZATION OF THE BOOK

This book is divided into three parts. Part I contains sets of problems on various topics. It is the heart of the book. Most problems should take you only a few minutes or less. If you cannot do a problem in 10 minutes, seek help from a tutor or from your instructor. Some of the problems point out pitfalls to avoid in your programs Other problems consist of two or more parts which look alike but which actually contain significant differences. Be on the alert so that you recognize the differences between these types of program segments. Occasionally, exercises are preceded by an asterisk (*) indicating that they contain advanced concepts that may be deferred until later on in the semester. Your instructor may organize his/her lectures in a different order than the chapters in this section and may therefore assign specific exercises for you to do.

Part II contains portions of old final examinations. Typically, a final exam at Brooklyn College consists of 75 points which are uniform for all students taking the first course, and 25 points from your own instructor. Near the end of the semester, you should test yourself on one of the portions of the final exams given here to see that you can not only do the problems but also that you can do them in the limited time available. You have about an hour and a half for the uniform portion; you should leave the other half hour for the 25 point problem from your instructor. The format of your final exam may differ from that which is given here. Ask your instructor whether additional sample final examinations are available.

Answers to some of the problems in Parts I and II are given in Part III. Do not look at the answers until you have seriously attempted the problems yourself. Otherwise, it is very easy to trick yourself into believing that you understand a concept when you see the answer; it may be a different matter when you have to generate the answer yourself. There is more than one way to do many computer assignments. If a method is presented in Part III which is different from your method, it is not necessarily true that your method is wrong. Compare the methods to see if you can tell why the printed answer is better, or worse, than yours. Are the methods equivalent? Will they both work with all kinds of data? If your answer is incorrect, try to learn from your mistake. You may learn a new algorithm from the answer given if you did not do the problem in the same way.

TYPES OF ERRORS

There are many types of errors in computer programming. *Syntax errors*, or *compilation errors*, which include the use of incorrect punctuation, incorrect keywords, etc., will be identified by the compiler during compilation. The Turbo C compiler will try to "guess" what error occurred but its guess is not necessarily correct. You can be sure that an error has been made at the point specified or immediately before that point. Knowing where the error is makes it easier to correct it and submit the program again. Never submit a program for grading which has errors in it.

A second type of error is an *execution* or *run-time error*. These errors involve asking the computer to do something which it cannot do. For example, if you ask the computer to divide by a variable which has a current value of zero, an execution error will result. The Turbo C compiler will show you where the error occurred, which is a big help in trying to correct it.

Logical errors are usually more difficult to find and more difficult to correct. These errors usually arise when the programmer does not understand the nature of the problem which is to be solved, or inadvertently gives the computer incorrect instructions to follow. For example, omitting the minus sign in a statement such as $x = -y;$ will be undetected by the computer. Unless some following use of the value produced (such as taking the square root of the answer) allows distinction between the value wanted and that produced, the computer has no way of telling that the minus sign has been omitted. However, an incorrect answer will be produced. You should check by hand at least several of the answers produced by the computer to see that your code is written correctly.

Some errors will not occur with some data, but will show up with other data. For example, if you want to take the square root of x, the correct answer may appear whenever x is positive but an error will occur when x is negative. Try to test your programs with a wide variety of values to ensure that they will work with all kinds of data.

An error frequently encountered is an infinite loop. Infinite loops are often generated by logical errors which have made the computer repeat a set of instructions again and again. You might see nothing at all happening at your computer. (The same symptom is produced when the computer is waiting for you to enter some data.) You might put some **printf** statements into your program temporarily so that some action is taken by the computer while it is in the loop, allowing you to diagnose what is happening. In fact, such temporary **printf** statements are an effective way to "debug" a program no matter what types of errors are involved.

ACKNOWLEDGMENTS

First and foremost, I would like to thank Professor David E. Goldberg and Professor Keith

Harrow my co-authors on previous versions of this book, *PL/I and PL/C Workbook*[1] and *Workbook for Pascal*[2] for permission to use many of the exercises in those books. In addition, Professor Harrow spent many additional hours proofreading early drafts of this book and offered many helpful suggestions. I am grateful to Professor Chaya Gurewitz for her many suggestions especially in the chapters involving pointers and structures. To my wife, Vivienne, and my children, I offer special thanks for their forbearance during the summer which was lost to them by my full time commitment to this book.

---

1 David   Goldberg, Keith Harrow, and Yedidyah Langsam, *PL/I and PL/C Workbook*, Prentice-Hall, New Jersey, 1984.
2 David   Goldberg, Keith Harrow, and Yedidyah Langsam, *Workbook for Pascal*, Brooklyn College Publications, New York, 1987.

PART I - PROBLEMS

CHAPTER 1 - BASIC PRINCIPLES

Section 1-1   Identifiers and Keywords (In Turbo C)

1.   What are the rules for naming identifiers in Turbo C?

2.   Select the valid identifiers from the following list. State why each of the others is not valid.

      (a) 123   (e) hunter
      (b) $50   (f) @60cents
      (c) 50dollars   (g) a_b
      (d) abc   (h) #define

3.   Select the valid identifiers from the following list. State why each of the others is not valid.

      (a) a/b   (e) $1.00
      (b) a-b   (f) $55
      (c) a_b   (g) m*n
      (d) a1.1   (h) IdEnTiFiEr

4.   Select the valid identifiers from the following list. State why each of the others is not valid.

      (a) a one   (e) best_student_in_class
      (b) number one   (f) non-integer
      (c) first class student (g) xrated
      (d) teacher's-pet

5.   Would the following identifiers be allowed in Turbo C? Would they be valid in all versions of C?

      (a) the_student_with_the_highest_grade_in_the_class
      (b) name_of_high_student
      (c) ScoreOfTheTopStudentInTheClass

6.   Select the valid identifiers in Turbo C from the following list. State why each of the others is not valid.

      (a) int   (e) printf

     (b) function   (f) while

     (c) for   (g) EOF

     (d) sizeof

7.   Which of the following pairs of identifiers would you choose for the number of students taking a course and the number of examinations taken by each student? (Note many of these pairs are legal, but not all are equally good. No one answer is **the** correct answer.)

        (a) x   y

        (b) s   e

        (c) students   exams

        (d) num_of_students   num_of_exams_per_student

        (e) num_of_students   exams/students

8.   A certain program is designed to find the name of a student who had the highest grade on an exam, and the score of that student. Which of the following pairs of identifiers, all of which are legal, would you choose for identifiers in your program? Explain why you made your choice.

        (a) x   y

        (b) hi   high

        (c) high_scorer   high_score

        (d) hi_scorer   high_grade

        (e) name_of_highest_student   grade_of_highest_student

        (f) curve_breaker   out_of_sight

9.   Explain the difference in C between a keyword and a **#define**d constant. Give two examples of each.

10.   Which of the following variable names are illegal, and why?

        (a) 4wayRadio   (e) helen123gold

        (b) happy birthday   (f) forloop

        (c) C.B.S.   (g) for

        (d) SwanSong   (h) loop

Section 1-2   Arithmetic Expressions

11.   How does the assignment operator (=) in C differ from the algebraic equal sign (=)?

12.   (a) How does the multiplication operator in C differ from that in algebra?
        (b) How does the division operator differ?

13.   Which if the following are incorrect C statements?

(a) x + 1 = y - 2;   (d) y = 2;
(b) x = x + 1;   (e) y = √2;
(c) x = x * n - 1;   (f) 2y = 14;

14.   In which of the following sets is the order of statements immaterial? That is, in which could you put the second or third statement first without any change in the final values of the variables after the segment is executed? **(sqrt(x)** is defined in the standard library *math.h* and returns the square root of **x**.)

(a) x = y;   (e) a = sqrt(b);
    w = z;   b = b * b;

(b) x = x + 1;   (f) z = x + 1;
    w = x + y;   y = x * x;

(c) printf("%d", x);   (g) z = sqrt(z);
    x = x + 1;   z = z * z;

(d) x = y;   (h) ++i;
    y = x;   printf("%d", i);

15.   Which of the following assignment statements may be inappropriate given that **number** has been declared as an **int** and **realno** has been declared as a **float**?

(a) number = 8;   (e) realno = 123.123;
(b) number = 8.25;   (f) number = realno;
(c) realno = 1;   (g) realno = number;
(d) realno = 1.0000E+00;   (h) realno = 9;

16.   For each of the following statements, if the statement is valid in C, then write "valid". If it is invalid, correct all the errors so that it becomes valid. Rewrite the entire corrected statement. Do not change things that are already valid. Change only the invalid parts.

```
#  include  {stdio.h}
/* comants */
void main()
{
        int x, y, 12y;
        x + 2 = 5;
        x = 3x + 7;
        if x > 10 printf("x is larger than 10");
        printf("\n%d %d", x, y);
} end main
```

17.   (a) Explain why an odd number is generated by the following program segment, no matter

what the value of **any_integer**. Assume that all variables are declared to have the data type **int**.

```
scanf("%d", &any_integer);
half = any_integer / 2;
odd_number = half * 2 + 1;
```

(b) Write a program which reads an arbitrary integer. It then prints the integer if it is even; otherwise it prints the number one less than the integer. For example, if 10 is read, 10 is printed because it is even, but if 9 is read, 8 is printed, since 8 is the even number one less than 9.

(c) Write a program which read an arbitrary integer. It then prints the closest number divisible by three which is equal to or greater than the original integer. For example, if 10 is read, 12 is printed, since it is the next highest integer divisible by 3. If 15 is read, then 15 is printed, since it is divisible by 3.

18.   What will be printed by the following program?

```
#include <stdio.h>
void main()
{
        int num;
        float realnum;

        num = 5;
        realnum = num;
        printf("%d %f\n", 1, 1.0);
        printf("%d %f\n", num, realnum);
        printf("%d\n", num * num);
        printf("%f\n", realnum * realnum);
        printf("%f\n", realnum * num);
        printf("%f\n", num * 1.0);
        printf("%d\n", num * 1);
        printf("%d\n", num * num * num);
        printf("%f\n", num * num * realnum);
}
```

19.   What output will be generated by the program below?

```
#include <stdio.h>
void main()
{
        int x, xx;
        float y, yy;
```

```
            x = 5;
            y = 7;
            xx = x / 2;
            printf("%d\n", xx);
            yy = y / 5.0;
            printf("%f\n", y);
            xx = x % 2;
            printf("%d\n", xx);
            yy = yy * y;
            printf("%f\n", yy);
            yy = yy + y;
            printf("%f\n", yy);
    }
```

20.   Write a program that reads a three-digit number, prints it out, and prints out the number with the digits in reverse order (e.g. 654 becomes 456).

21.   Assume that an integer variable called **zip** contains a 5-digit integer representing a zip code in the eastern part of the country. Write the C statements and the variable declarations needed to extract the middle digit out of the zip. The output should read: "The middle digit of xxyxx is y" (where xxyxx is the integer in **zip** and y is the middle digit of that integer). Thus if **zip** were 12345, then the output would be "The middle digit of 12345 is 3."

Section 1-3   Arithmetic Precedence

22.   What are the arithmetic precedence rules in C?

23.   What values are printed by the following program?

```
        #include <stdio.h>
        void main()
        {
                int m, n;

                n = 10;
                m = n + (6 / 2);
                printf("%d\n", m);
                m = (n + 6) / 2;
                printf("%d\n", m);
                m = n + 6 / 2;
                printf("%d\n", m);
        }
```

24.   Evaluate the following C expressions:

      (a) 5 + 3 * 4   (b) 12 / 4 * 2

25.   What values will be established by the following assignment statements? All variables are declared to be of type **int**.

        value_1 = 2 + 4 * 6 / 3 + 4;
        value_2 = 2 + (4 * 2) / (3 + 4);
        value_3 = (2 + 4) * 2 / (3 + 4);

26.   In each of the following sets of assignment statements, which statements, if any, would yield the same value for **y**? The value of **x** is the same throughout the whole exercise (for example, **x = 15.5**). Both **x** and **y** are declared to be of type **float**.

    (1) (a) y = (3 + 2) * 4;   (3) (a) y = x * 4 / 4 * x;
        (b) y = 3 + 2 * 4;   (b) y = x * 4 / x * 4;
        (c) y = 3 + (2 * 4);   (c) y = (x * 4) / x * 4);
                              (d) y = x * 4 / (x * 4);
    (2) (a) y = (x + 2)/(x - 2);   (e) y = (x * 4) / (x * 4);
        (b) y = x + 2 / x - 2;
        (c) y = (x + 2) / x - 2;

27.   Write a C assignment statement for each of these algebraic expressions:

    (a) $y = \dfrac{ab - a^2}{xy^3}$ (b) $y = \dfrac{a(1+b)}{x+1}$ (c) $y = \dfrac{a + (1+b)^2}{2a}$

    (d) $y = \dfrac{6\frac{a}{b} + 1}{x - x^2}$ (e) $y = 6a - 2b$ (f) $y = 2x^3$

    (g) $y = (2x)^3$ (h) $y = 2(x)^3$ (i) $y = -x^2$

    (j) $y = (-x)^2$ (k) $y = -(x)^2$

28.   Write a C assignment statement equivalent to the expression given below:

$$y = \frac{-b - \sqrt{b^2 - 4ac}}{2a}$$

29.   Indicate the output expected from the following program:

```
#include <stdio.h>
void main()
{
        int x, y, z;

        x = 2 + 3 / (4 - 1);
        y = 10 * 3 * 3;
        z = (1 + 4) / 5 * 2;
        printf("%d  %d  %d\n", x, y, z);

}
```

30.   Write a C assignment statement equivalent to each of the expressions given below. Use as few pairs of parentheses as necessary without changing the meaning of the expression.

$$x = \frac{a + 2b}{c - 3d^4} \qquad\qquad x = \frac{a + 2b^2}{3cd^4}$$

31.   Indicate the output expected from the following program:

```
#include <stdio.h>
void main()
{
        int x, y, z;

        x = 5 + 2 / 3 - 4;
        y = (14 + 7) / 7 * 10;
        z = (-8) * (-8);
        printf("%d  %d  %d\n", x, y, z);

}
```

32.   Write a C statement corresponding to each of the expressions below. Use as few pairs of parentheses as necessary without changing the meaning of the expression.

$$x = \frac{2a + b}{3c} \qquad\qquad x = 2a + b / 3c$$

33.   What output will be generated by the following program?

```
#include <stdio.h>
void main()
{
```

```
            int b, c, d, f;
            float x;

            x = 10;
            b = 2;
            c = 5;
            d = 8;
            f = 2;
            x = 8 - c / b + d % f * c + 1;
            printf("%f\n", x);
       }
```

34.   Write C statements to translate each of the following algebraic equations:

(a) $y = \dfrac{x+1}{x-1}$ (b) $z = \dfrac{x-4xy+y}{x-y}$

(c) $a = \sqrt{r}$ (d) $x = \dfrac{-b+\sqrt{b^2-4ac}}{2a}$

(e) $w = |x+y|/x$

35.   Write a C statement that corresponds to the following mathematical formula:

$$y = \dfrac{x^2+7x-1}{\dfrac{x}{3}}$$

36.   Evaluate **g**, **h**, **i**, and **j**, assuming that each variable has been declared to be of type **float**.

```
            a = 3;
            b = 2;
            c = 4;
            g = (a + b * c) / (a - b);
            h = - a - b + c;
            i  = -(b * b);
            j  = 100 * a - 10 * b + c;
```

37.   What is the value assigned to **x** after each statement is executed? The variable **x** has been declared to be of type **float**.

(a) x = 10 + 8 / 2 * 2 - 4 * 2;
(b) x = 5 + (4 * (3 - 2)) * 2;

38.   Translate the following equations into C. Do not use any unnecessary parentheses. All variables have been declared to be of type **float**.

$$\text{(a)} \quad s = \frac{x - 3xy + 1}{\dfrac{x + y}{x - y}} \qquad\qquad \text{(b)} \quad s = \frac{b - 4ac}{2a}$$

39.   What is the value assigned to **x** after each statement is executed? Assume that **x** has been declared to be of type **float**.

(a) x = 5 + 4 * (3 - 2) * 10;
(b) x = 10 + 8 / 2 * (2 - 4) * 2;
(c) x = 9 * 7 / 3 + 6 / 2 * 3 + 7;

40.   (a) For the series of statements shown below, show what will be stored in variables **a**, **b**, and **c**.

```
int a, b, c;
   ...
a = 6;
b = a + 7 / 5;
c = (a * b) % 4;
```

(b) Evaluate **x** according to the C precedence rules and then show exactly what is printed.

```
float x, b, c, d, f, g, h;
      ...
d = 6;
c = 6;
f = 2;
b = 3;
g = 1 / 2;
h = 6;
x = -b + d * c / f * g + h;
printf("x = %f\n", x);
```

41.*   Evaluate **g**, **h**, and **i**, assuming that each variable has been declared to be of type **int**.

```
a = 2;
b = 3;
c = 4;
```

```
b++;
g = 5 + a++;
h = 5 + ++c;
i = ++g + h++;
```

42.*   What will be the values of each of the variables after the following program segment is executed?

```
int a, b, c, x, y, z;
        ...
x = (a = 3) + (b = 4);
y = (c=5) - b++;
z = a + b +c;
```

43.   Indicate the output expected from the following program:

```
#include <stdio.h>
void main()
{
        int x=1, y=2, z=3;

        x += 1;
        y++;
        z *= x + y;
        printf("%d  %d  %d\n", x, y, z);
}
```

44.*   What output will be generated by the following program?

```
#include <stdio.h>
void main()
{
        int a, b, c, d, e=6, f;

        a = 1;
        b = 2;
        c = 5;
        d = 8;
        f = 2;
        a += ++b + ++c;
        d -= e-- - f--;
        printf("%d %d %d %d %d %d\n", a, b, c, d, e, f);
}
```

45.*   What values will be established by the following assignment statements? All variables are declared to be of type **int**.

```
i = j = k = 0;
++i;
j++;
k += i + j;
l = ++i + j++;
```

46.*   What output will be generated by the following program?

```
#include <stdio.h>
void main()
{
        int a, b, c, d, e=6, f;

        a = 1;
        b = 2;
        c = a > 0 ? 5: 10;
        d = a == 5 ? d = a + b: 0;
        f = b < 10? a++: b++;
        printf("%d %d %d %d %d %d\n", a, b, c, d, e, f);
}
```

Section 1-4   Scientific Notation

47.   What does the **E** (or **e**) mean in the printout of a real number?

48.   Write in decimal form (using the **%f** format item) the value of each of the following numbers as printed by the computer:

1.000000e+02	-4.000000e-01	7.000000e-03
2.500000E-01	-5.000000E+00	8.888880E+04
3.000000e+00	-6.000000e-02	-9.000000e-04

49.   Write in decimal form the value of each of the following numbers which might be included in assignment statements in a program. Compare the values on each line. Are they the same in each set?

(a) 1.00e0	1:00e+00	1.00e-00
(b) 2.00E+02	2.00E2	2.00E+2
(c) 3.00e-03	3.00e-3	3.00e3
(d) 4.00e-05	4.00e-5	-4.00e5
(e) -5.000E-1	5.00E1	-5.00E1

50.   (a) Write each of the following numbers in floating point format in a form which would be permitted in an assignment statement.

$\qquad$ (i) -1.0×10^{-1} $\qquad$ (v) 500×10^3

$\qquad$ (ii) 2000 $\qquad$ (vi) 6.02×10^{23}

$\qquad$ (iii) 0.030 $\qquad$ (vii) 7.0×10^{11}

$\qquad$ (iv) 4.0×10^{-3}

(b) Rewrite each of the above numbers (using the **%e** format item) in the format in which the computer would print them out.

51.   (a) Express the following numbers in floating point notation (normalized form).

$\qquad$ -1500 $\qquad\qquad\qquad$ 0.00702

(b) Express in ordinary decimal (fixed point) form:

$\qquad$ 6.666e+04

52.   Change the following numbers to ordinary decimal (fixed point) form.

$\qquad$ -1.23e-2 $\qquad\qquad$ -8.00e04
$\qquad$ 1.00e00 $\qquad\qquad$ 1.23456e-01
$\qquad$ 1.00E02 $\qquad\qquad$ 1.6E-8
$\qquad$ 4.0E-02 $\qquad\qquad$ -8.00E4
$\qquad$ 20e2 $\qquad\qquad\quad$ 0.00234e3

53.   Change the following numbers to floating point form:

$\qquad$ 1000 $\qquad\qquad$ 0.00603 $\qquad\qquad$ -0.06
$\qquad$ 1.23 $\qquad\qquad$ 0.10 $\qquad\qquad\quad$ -678
$\qquad$ 60.4 $\qquad\qquad$ -1400 $\qquad\qquad$ 1000000
$\qquad$ 1×10^{10} $\qquad\quad$ 1.6×10^{-9} $\qquad\quad$ 6.02×10^{23}

54.   What would be printed by the following program? Run this program to verify your answer.

```
#include <stdio.h>
void main()
{
```

```
        if (0.4 + 0.1 == 0.5)
                printf("no truncation\n");
        else
                printf("truncation\n");
        printf("%f\n", 0.4 + 0.1);
}
```

55.   What would be printed by the following program? Run this program to verify your
       answer.

```
#include <stdio.h>
void main()
{
        if (0.25 + 0.25 == 0.5)
                printf("no truncation\n");
        else
        printf("truncation\n");
        printf("%f\n", 0.25 + 0.25);
}
```

Section 1-5   Standard (*math.h*) Library Functions

56.   What do the standard *math.h* library functions **sqrt**, **abs**, **ceil**, **floor**, and **pow** do?

57.   Tell what is wrong with the following program segment:

```
sqrt(x) = 7;
sin(z) = 0.5;
```

58.   What will be printed by the following program segment?

```
#include <stdio.h>
#include <math.h>
void main()
{
        int w, x;
        float y;

        w = 4;
        x = abs(w - 5);
        y = sqrt(x);
        printf("%d  %d  %f\n", w, x, y);
}
```

59.   What is printed by the following program segment?

```
#include <stdio.h>
#include <math.h>
void main()
{
        float x, y, a, b, c, d;

        x = 2;
        y = 4;
        a = x * y / x + y;
        b = sqrt(x);
        c = x / y * (y + 1);
        d = (x * x + y) / ((x - y) * (x - y));
        printf("%f  %f\n", a, b);
        printf("%f  %f\n", c, d);
}
```

60.   What would be printed by the following program?

```
#include <stdio.h>
#include <math.h>
void main()
{
        int i = 1;

        while ( i % 7 != 0) {
                if ( i % 2 == 0)
                        printf("%d  %f\n", i, sqrt(i));
                i++;
        }
}
```

61.   What is the value of **y** in part (a) and **min** in part (b)? (Assume that **z** has a value before the execution of part (b).)

```
float x, y, z, min;
```

(a)   x = 2;
        y = sqrt(x * x + 5);

(b)   if (z * z < 0)
                min = z * z;
        else
                min = 0;

62.   If **n** has data type **int**, what will be the value of **n** after each of these statements is executed?

```
n = 11 % 4;
n = 17 / 3;
n = floor(M_PI);    /* M_PI is a Turbo C predefined constant in math.h */
                    /* equal to 3.14159                                */
```

63.   What are the results of the following program?

```
#include <stdio.h>
#include <math.h>
void main()
{
        float x, y;
        int n, m;

        x = 10.5;
        n = x;
        printf("%d  %f\n", n, x);
        x = n;
        printf("%d  %f\n", n, x);
        x = n + 1.5;
        n = x + 1.5;
        printf("%d  %f\n", n, x);
        printf("%d  %f\n", n, ceil(x));
}
```

64.   What output would have been produced if the **floor** function would have been used in the last problem instead of the **ceil** function?

65.   Is the following assignment statement legal? If not, why?

```
sqrt = sqrt(x);
```

66.   Write a program that read a real number which represents a weight in pounds and expresses the weight in terms of pounds and ounces. For example, 5.20 pounds becomes 5 pounds 3 ounces.

67.   Write a program to print the cost in dollars of a first-class package, for which the price is 33 cents for the first ounce or fraction and 17 cents for each additional ounce or fraction. Assume that postal scales read to the nearest hundredth of an ounce.

68.   What will be printed by each of the following programs? Explain why negative numbers

may be printed.

(a)   #include <stdio.h>
        void main()
        {
                int num;

                num = 50;
                printf("%d\n", num * num * num);
                printf("%d\n", num * num * num / 1.0);
                printf("%f\n", 1.0 * num * num * num);
                printf("%d\n", 1 * num * num * num);
                printf("%f\n", num * num * 1.0 * num);
        }

(b)   #include <stdio.h>
        void main()
        {
                int cube, num;
                float fcube;

                num = 50;
                cube = num * num * num;
                fcube = num * num * num;
                printf("%d   %10.0f\n", cube, fcube);
        }

(c)   #include <stdio.h>
        void main()
        {
                int num;
                float floatnum;

                num = 50;
                floatnum = num;
                printf("%d\n", num * num * floatnum);
                printf("%f\n", num * num * floatnum);
        }

CHAPTER 2 - CONDITIONAL BRANCHING

Section 2-1 *if* and *if-else* Statements

1. What is the value of **x** after the following program segment is executed?

    ```
    int x;
        ...
    x = 7;
    if (x % 3 < 1)
            x = x + 2;
    ```

2. Write a C statement to accomplish each of the following:

    (a) set **q** equal to the square root of 15 if **v** is negative;
    (b) set **h** to 3 if **count** is a multiple of 10;
    (c) set **z** equal to the integer closest to the real number 4.67 if **q** is not equal to 0.
    (d) set **i** equal to 7 if **x** is not negative or to 8 otherwise.

3.   What will be printed by each of the following program segments? Use the following declaration and **scanf** statement for each part. Use the following pairs of test data:

    2 3   3 3   4 3

    ```
    int a, b;
        ...
    scanf("%d  %d", &a, &b);
    ```

    (a) ```
         if (a < b)
                 printf("A LOWER");
         else
                 printf("A NOT LOWER");
         ```

    (b)  ```
         if (a <= b)
                 printf("A NOT HIGHER")
         else
                 printf("A HIGHER");
         ```

    (c) ```
         if (a != b)
                 printf("NOT EQUAL");
         else
                 printf("EQUAL");
         ```
         ```

4.   Explain why the message "A HIGHER" would be inappropriate for the **else** clause in
       problem 3(a).

5.   Criticize the following statement. Write a simpler statement which has the same effect.

```
if (a > b)
        c = 12;
else
        c = 12;
```

6.   Which variables in the following program segment must be initialized before the
       assignment statements shown?

```
int a, b, c, d, e, f, g, h, i, j, k;
        ...
a = b * b;
if (c == d)
        e = f;
else
        g = h;
i = i + 1;
j = abs(k);
```

7.   A parcel delivery service charges according to the following rate schedule:

up to 14 ounces	0.45 per ounce or part of an ounce
over 14 ounces	0.36 per ounce or part over 14 ounces
minimum charge	3.00

Note that a fraction of an ounce must be charged for as a complete ounce. Write a
complete C program which will read the weight of a package (in ounces) and print the
cost of sending the package.

For example, if the weight is 16.3 ounces, the cost should be

6.30	(14 × 0.45 for the first 14 ounces)
+1.08	(3 × 0.36 for the 2.3 ounces above 14 ounces)
────	
7.38	The total cost for the package.

If the weight were 4.1 ounces, the cost would be calculated to be 2.25, but the minimum
charge is 3.00. The program should print 3.00 for this package.

8.*   Eliminate the conditional operator (?) from the following expressions:

(a)   `x > 0 ? a = 5 : a = 10;`   (b)   `a = x > 0 ? 5 : 10;`

(c)   `a = x > 5 && x < 10 ? a + 1 : a - 1`   (d)   `a = 5 + (x > 0 ? 1 : 0);`

Section 2-2   Nested *if-else*

9.   Simplify:

(a)
```
if (a >b)
        printf("%d", a);
else
        printf("%d", a);
```

(b)
```
if (a > b)
{
        if (c > d)
                e = 12;
}
```

(c)
```
if (a > b)
{
        if (c > d)
                e = 12;
        else
                e = 19;
}
```

10.   Criticize and improve the indentation in the following program segments:

(a)
```
if (x > y )
        a = b;
        c = d;
        e = f;
```

(b)
```
if (a == b) if (c == d) e = f;
else e = f + 2;
```

(c)
```
if (a == b) if (c == d) e = f;
else    ;    else e = f + 2;
```

(d)
```
if (a == b) {
        c = d;
        e = f;
}
else {
        c = d + 1;
        e = f + 1;
}
```

11.   Simplify each of the following segments:

(a)   **if** (a > z) {
              x++;
        }
        else {
              x = y + z;
        }

(b)   **if** (a > z) {
              if (b > y) {
                    x = 2;
              }
              else {
                    x = 7;
              }
        }

12.   Show what will be printed by the following C statements:

```
int a, b, c, d, e;
    ...
a = 3;
b = 5;
c = 7;
d = 4;
e = 2;
if (a < b || d > e)
        if (b > c && c > d)
                printf("win\n");
        else    if (d < e)
                        printf("place\n");
                else
                        printf("show\n");
```

13.   (a) What output will be produced by the following program? Note: Do *not* use the "style" represented by this segment in any of your own programs!

```
#include <stdio.h>
void main()
{
        int a, b, c;

        a = 5;
        b = 6;
        c = 7;
        if (a == b) if (c == b + 1) printf("green\n"); else
        printf("blue\n"); else printf("red\n");

        if (a == b - 1) if (c == b + 1) printf("green\n"); else
        printf("blue\n"); else printf("red\n");
}
```

(b) The logic of the above program is difficult to follow because of the way the code appears. Rewrite the program (without changing the syntax) so that the logic is easier to follow.

14.   Rewrite each of the following program segments with proper indentation, and then state what output will be produced by each segment. Note: Do *not* use the "style" represented in these segments in any of your own programs!

```
int a = 4, b = 3, c = 2, d = 2, e = 1;
```

(a)   `if (a > b) if (c > d) e = e + 3; else; else e = e + 10;`
       `printf("e = %d", e);`

(b)   `if (a > b) if (c > d) e = e + 3; else e = e + 10;`
       `printf("e = %d", e);`

(c)   `if (a > b) if (c > d) e = e + 3;`
              `else e = e + 10;`
       `printf("e = %d", e);`

Section 2-3   Logical and Relational Operators

15.   Simplify each of the following segments of code:

(a)   `if (a > 5 || a == 5)`
              `x = 66;`

(b)   `x = 99;`
       `if (x > 33)`
              `y = 6;`

16.   Write the following program segments more efficiently, and using better style:

(a)   `if (!(a >=b)) x = 7; else x = -5;`

(b)   `if (a == b)`
              `;`
       `else`
              `a = b;`

(c)   `if (a != b)`
              `a = b;`

17.   Rewrite the following program segment (a) without any logical operators. (b) with a
        logical **not** operator.

```
if (a != b)
        x = 5;
else
        x = -5;
```

18.   Show what will be printed by the following C statements.

```
int a, b, c, d, e;

a = 1;
b = 18;
c = 6;
d = 42;
e = 8;
if (!(a == b && c * c <= 100 || d != e / 8))
        printf("valid\n");
else
        printf("invalid\n");
if (1000 > a + b * b * 10 || !(e * d == a / d))
        a = a + b;
else
        a = a - b;
printf("%d\n", a);
```

19.   Which of the lettered statements, (a) or (b), is equivalent to

```
if (a > b && c > d || e > f) ...
```

(a)   `if ((a > b && c > d) || e > f)  ...`
(b)   `if (a > b && (c > d || e > f))  ...`

20.   What will be printed by the following program segment?

```
int x, y, z;
 ...
x = 3;
y = 8;
z = 10;
if ( x ==y || z > x + y)
        if (y < z)
                z = 5;
        else
```

```
                      z = 6;
        else    if (x < z)
                          z++;
                else
                          z = z + 10;
        printf("%d  %d  %d\n", x, y, z);
```

21.   What will be printed by the following program?

```
        #include <stdio.h>
        void main()
        {
                int a , b, c, d, e;

                a = 4; b = 3; c = 2; d = 2; e = 1;
                if ( a > b && c > d)
                        e = e + 3;
                else
                        e = e + 10;
                printf("e = %d\n", e);

                a = 4; b = 3; c = 2; d = 2; e = 1;
                if ( a > b || c > d)
                        e = e + 3;
                else
                        e = e + 10;
                printf("e = %d\n", e);

                a = 3; b = 3; c = 2; d = 2; e = 1;
                if ( a > b || c > d)
                        e = e + 3;
                else
                        e = e + 10;
                printf("e = %d\n", e);

                a = 3; b = 3; c = 2; d = 2; e = 1;
                if ( a > b && c > d)
                        e = e + 3;
                else
                        e = e + 10;
                printf("e = %d\n", e);

                a = 4; b = 3; c = 2; d = 2; e = 1;
                if (!(a > b) && c > d)
                        e = e + 3;
```

```
          else
                  e = e + 10;
          printf("e = %d\n", e);

          a = 4; b = 3; c = 2; d = 2; e = 1;
          if (!(a > b) || c > d)
                  e = e + 3;
          else
                  e = e + 10;
          printf("e = %d\n", e);

          a = 3; b = 3; c = 2; d = 2; e = 1;
          if ( a > b || !(c > d))
                  e = e + 3;
          else
                  e = e + 10;
          printf("e = %d\n", e);

          a = 3; b = 3; c = 2; d = 2; e = 1;
          if ( a > b && !(c > d))
                  e = e + 3;
          else
                  e = e + 10;
          printf("e = %d\n", e);
}
```

22.   Rewrite the following program segments without using the logical **not** operator:

(a)   **if** (x != y)
               x++;
       else
               x--;

(b)   **if** (!(grade >= 0) || !(grade <= 100))
               printf("GRADE INVALID")
       else
               total = total + grade;

(c)   **if** (a != b)
               ;
       else
               c = d;

(d)   **if** (!(a >=b) && !(c >=d) || !(c >= e))
               x = 1;

```
        else
              x = 2;
```

23.   Rewrite the following program segment using only one **if-else**:

```
        if (a > b)
              e = e + 3;
        else   if (c > d)
                    e = e + 3;
              else
                    e = e + 10;
```

24.   Criticize the following program segments:

```
        #define TRUE 1
        #define FALSE 0
```

(a)   **if** (grade <= 100 || grade >= 0)
              grade_is_valid = TRUE;

(b)   **if** (grade < 0 && grade > 100)
              grade_is_valid = FALSE;

25.   Improve each of the following program segments:

(a)   **if** (a > b)
              x = 1;
        if (c < d)
              x = 1;
        if (e == f)
              x = 1;

(b)   **if** (a == b)
              if (c > d)
                    if (e > f)
                          printf("%d", x);

(c)   **if** (a > b) {
              y = x;
              w = x -1;
        }
        else {
              y = x;
              w = x + 1;
        }

26.   What will be the values of x, y, and z after execution of the following program segment?

```
int a = 5, b = 5, c = 4, d = 4, e = 2, f = 1;
int x, y, z;
    ...

if ((a > b && c > d) || e > f)
      x = 15;
else
      x = 20;

if (a > b && (c > d || e > f))
      y = 15;
else
      y = 20;
            .
if (a > b && c > d || e > f)
      z = 15;
else
      z = 20;
```

27.   What is printed by the following program?

```
#include <stdio.h>
void main()
{
      int a, b, c, d;

      a = 6;
      b = 4;
      c = 9;
      d = 9;
      if (a == b || b == 5) {
            c = a - b * a;
            b = b - 1;
      }
      else    if (b == 4)
                    a = a;
              else {
                    b = 10 * (a - 1);
                    d = a + b * a - b;
                    if (a > b)
                          c = d + 1;
```

```
                        else
                                c = b + 2;
                    }
                printf("%d  %d  %d  %d", a, b, c, d);
            }
```

28.   (a) Distinguish between the following two program segments:

(i) **if** (x != 0 && y/x == 100)   (ii) **if** (y/x == 100 && x != 0)
...   ...

(b) What would happen if **x** were zero?

29.   Given the following values, for each of the conditions given below describe how much of the condition would be evaluated.

int x = 0, y = 1, c = 2:

(a)   if (x == y || x == c) ...

(b)   if (x == y && x ==c) ...

(c)   if (x == 0 || x == y) ...

(d)   if (x != y || y == c && x != 0) ...

(e)   if (x != y && y == c || x != 0) ...

Section 2-4   Integer and Logical Values

30.   (a) What value is used by C to represent an expression which is logically *true*?
(b) What value is used by C to represent an expression which is logically *false*?
(c) When evaluating a logical expression, what is the logical meaning of a positive number? a negative number? zero?

31.   For each of the following, give the value of the expression and its logical interpretation. For example, the statement x = 5; has a value of 5 and a logical interpretation of *true*, and the expression 5 > 6 has a value of 0 and a logical interpretation of *false*. Assume the following declaration:

int x = 0, y = 1, c = 2;

(a)   6 > 5 + 1   (f)   x >= y && c = 2

(b)   x = 0;

(c)   x == 0;

(d)   15

(e)   x = 5 - 10;

(g)   -25

(h)   c = x == 0;

(i)   x--;

(j)   x >= y && c = 2

32.   Simplify the following expressions, in which the variables are declared to have the data type **int**. Assume the following preprocessor statements:

```
#define TRUE 1
#define FALSE 0
```

(a)   **if** (switch == TRUE) ...

(b)   **if** (switch == FALSE) ...

(c)   **if** (sw1 == TRUE && sw2 == FALSE) ...

33.   Explain the following assignment statement, in which **a** and **b** have been declared to be of the same type (e.g., both **int** or both **float**) and **flag** has been declared to be of type **int**.

```
flag = a == b;
```

34.   What will be printed by the following program?

```
#include <stdio.h>
void main()
{
        int a, b;

        a = 2;
        b = a;
        printf("%d  %d  %d  %d\n", a, b, a = b, a == b);
}
```

35.*   What output will be produced by the following program?

```
#include <stdio.h>
#include <math.h>
#include <string.h>
void main()
{
        int a, b, c, d, tf;
        char cat[5], dog[5];

        strcpy(cat,"meow");
```

```
        strcpy(dog,"bark");
        a = 5;
        b = 6;
        c = 11;
        d = 1;
        tf = a == b;
        printf("%d\n", tf);

        tf = c % d == a / b && a < b;
        printf("%d\n", tf);

        tf = abs(a - b) == d * -1 && c - b == a + b
                || c / b == b / a;
        printf("%d\n", tf);

        tf = abs(a - b) == d * -1 || c - b == a + b
                && c / b == b / a;
        printf("%d\n", tf);

        if (strcmp(cat, dog) > 0)
                printf("true\n");
        else
                printf("nonsense\n");

        if (strcmp("cat", "dog") > 0)
                printf("true\n");
        else
                printf("nonsense\n");
}
```

36.   Show exactly what will be printed by this program.

```
        #include <stdio.h>
        #define TRUE 1
        #define FALSE 0
        void main()
        {
                int a, b, c, d, e;

                a = b = d =TRUE;
                c = e = FALSE;
                if (a && b || c)
                        printf("true\n");
                else
                        printf("false\n");
```

```
            if (!(d || c || a) && !c)
                    printf("true\n");
            else
                    printf("false\n");
            if (!c || (d && e))
                    printf("true\n");
            else
                    printf("false\n");
        }
```

37.   Construct a truth table for each of the following logical expressions. Assume **a**, **b**, and **c** have been declared to be of type **int**.

(a)   a && !b || c

(b)   !(a && b) || c

(c)   (a || b) && !(a && c)

CHAPTER 3 - FLOWCHARTS

1.   Write C program segments corresponding to the flowcharts in Figure 3-1.

Figure 3-1   Flowcharts for Translation to C

(a)

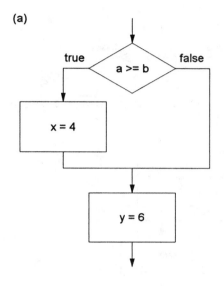

(b)

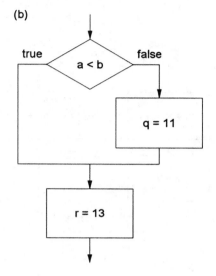

(c)

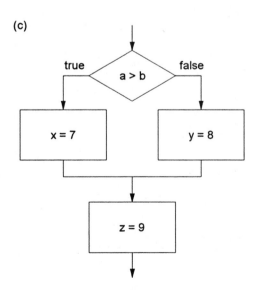

2.   Write C program segments corresponding to the flowcharts in Figure 3-2.

Figure 3-2   Flowcharts for Translation to C

(a)

(b)

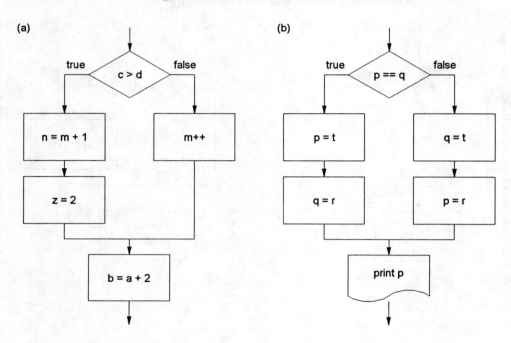

(c)

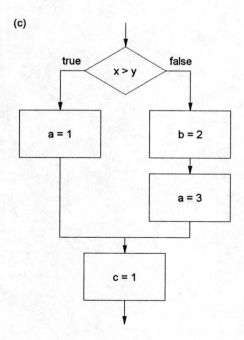

3. Amend the flowcharts in Figure 3-3 to improve the style or logic. Then write C program segments corresponding to the ammended flowcharts.

Figure 3-3   Flowcharts for Analysis

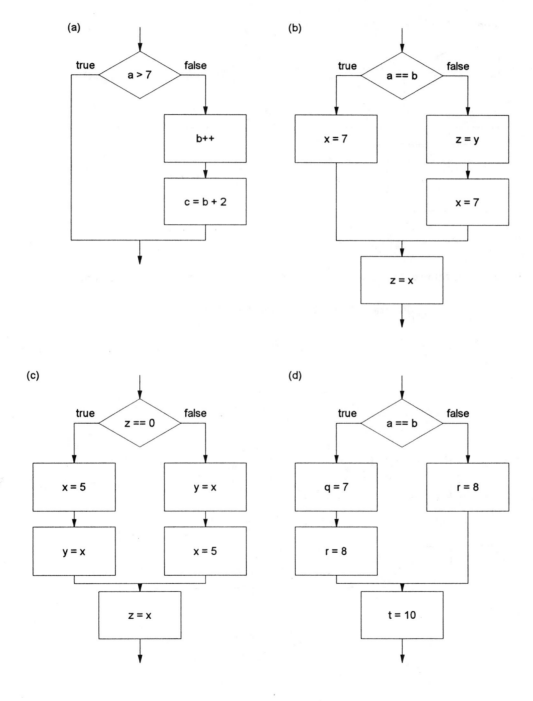

Figure 3-3   Flowcharts for Analysis (continued)

(e)   (f)

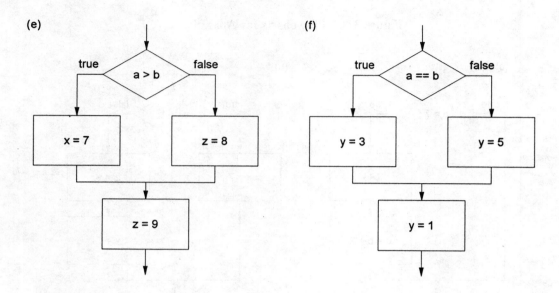

4.   Write C program segments corresponding to the flowcharts in Figures 3-4 and 3-5.

Figure 3-4   Flowchart for Translation to C

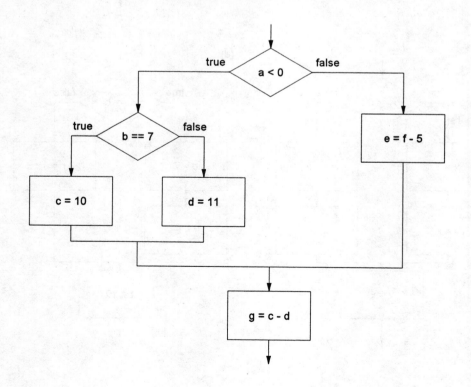

Figure 3-5   Flowchart for Translation to C

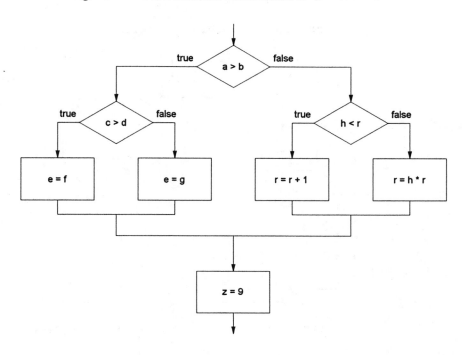

5.   Write a C program segment corresponding to the flowchart in Figure 3-6 with an **if-else** construction. Repeat using the **abs** function in the standard *math.h* library instead.

Figure 3-6   Flowchart for Analysis

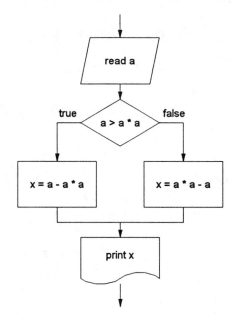

6.   Write a C program segment corresponding to the flowchart in Figure 3-7.

Figure 3-7   Flowchart for Translation to C

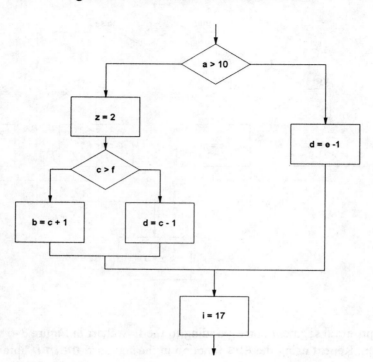

7.   Study the flowcharts in Figure 3-8. If it is possible to improve the logic in a flowchart, amend it. Then write a program segment for each amended or original flowchart.

Figure 3-8   Flowcharts for Analysis

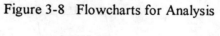

(a)

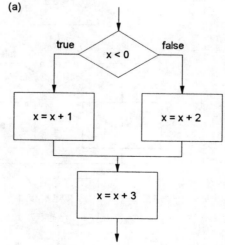

Figure 3-8 Flowcharts for Analysis (continued)

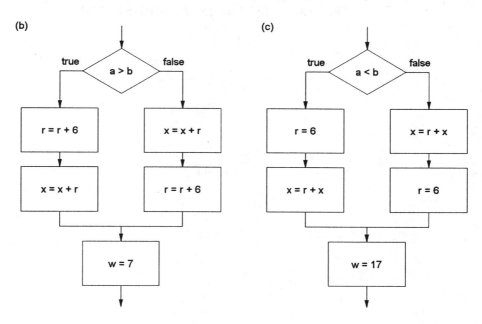

8. Write a C program segment corresponding to the flowchart shown in Figure 3-9.

9. Write C program segments corresponding to the flowcharts in Figure 3-10 using nested **if** or **if-else** constructions. Repeat using only a single **if** or **if-else.**

10. Translate the flowchart in Figure 3-11 into C code.

11. Consider the flowchart shown in Figure 3-4. Write a C program segment corresponding to that flowchart:

(a) if the statement **d = 11;** were not present. (That is, if **b** does not equal 7, do nothing.)

(b) if the statement **e = f - 5;** were not present but **d = 11;** were still present.

(c) In which of these cases is a null **else** required? Could a null **else** be used in both cases? Explain.

12. Consider the flowchart in Figure 3-7. Write a C program segment corresponding to the flowchart

(a) if the statement **d = e - 1;** were not present.
(b) if the statement **d = c - 1;** were not present, instead.
(c) Would a null **else** be required in either of these cases?

Figure 3-9   Flowchart for Translation to C

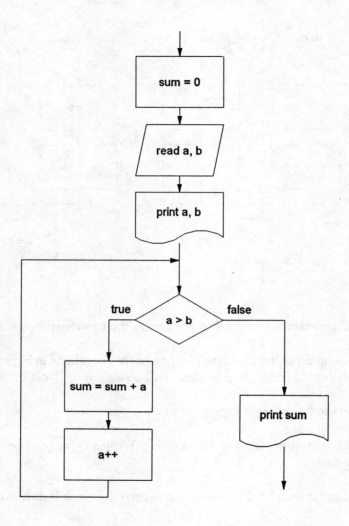

Figure 3-10   Flowcharts for Analysis

(a)

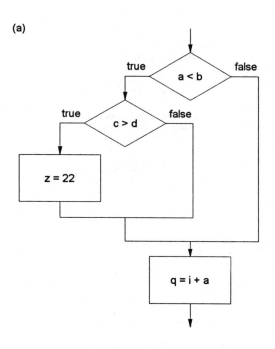

(b)

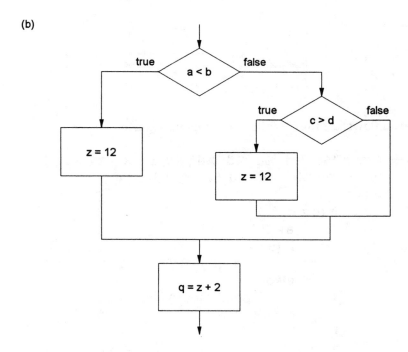

Figure 3-11   Flowchart for Analysis

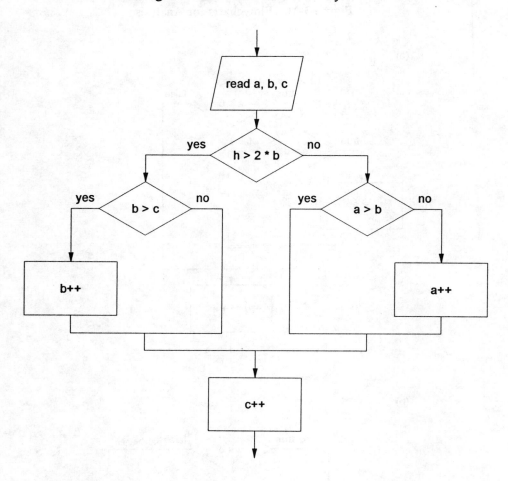

13.   Draw a flowchart for the following program segment.

```
scanf("%d %d %d %d %d", &a, &b, &c, &x, &y);
printf("%d %d %d %d %d\n", a, b, c, x, y);
if (x == y)
        if (c > d) {
                .a = 2 * b;
                if (a == x)
                        printf("yes\n");
                else
                        printf("no\n");
                c = c + 1;
        }
        else

                ;
```

```
else    if (x > y) {
                a = 2 * c;
                printf("%d  %d\n", x, y);
        }
        else    if (x == a)
                        printf("maybe\n");
if (c > x)
        c = x;
printf("enough\n");
```

CHAPTER 4 - LOOP STRUCTURES

Section 4-1 *while* **Loops**

1.   Show exactly what is printed by the following program.

```
#include <stdio.h>
void main()
{
        int x, y;

        x = 4;
        y = 1;
        while (x < 5) {
                x = x + y / 3;
                y = y + 1;
                printf("x = %d    y = %d\n", x, y);
        }
        printf("the sum of x and y is %d\n", x + y);
}
```

2.   What is the difference between the two programs shown below? Assume that the value 5 is read from input in each case.

(a)
```
#include <stdio.h>
void main()
{
        int x;

        scanf("%d", &x);
        if (x > 2)
                x = x -1;
        printf("%d", x);
}
```

(b)
```
#include <stdio.h>
void main()
{
        int x;

        scanf("%d", &x);
        while (x > 2)
                x = x -1;
        printf("%d", x);
}
```

3.   What values are printed by the following program? Use the data shown below.

```
#include <stdio.h>
#include <string.h>
void main()
{
        char a[10], b[10];
        int j;
```

```
                    j = 0;
                    scanf("%s", a);
                    while (strcmp(a, "zzzzz") != 0) {
                            scanf("%s", b);
                            if (strlen(a) > strlen(b))
                                    printf("A WINNER\n");
                            else
                                    printf("B WINNER\n");
                            j++;
                            scanf("%s", a);
                    }
                    printf("%d\n", j);
            }

    data:   MEM1
              MEM2
            DROOL12345
            SPOCK
            DROOL
            SPOCKSPOCK
            zzzzz
```

4.   What would be the result of running the above program if the last line of the data
       contained 4 z's rather than the 5 shown above?

5.   (a) What is the result of the following program? Assume the user enters a control-z (^Z)
       after entering the data items shown below. (b) How does it avoid the potential error
       alluded to in Question 4?

```
            #include <stdio.h>
            void main()
            {
                    int x, y, pairs = 0;

                    while (scanf("%d  %d", &x, &y) ==2) {
                        if (x > y)
                                printf("1st is larger\n");
                        else
                                printf("1st is not larger\n");
                        pairs++;
                    }
                    printf("%d pairs were processed\n", pairs);
            }

    data:   23      21
```

```
                          1        0
                         15        5
                         20       -2
                         -4        6
```

6.   What would be the result of the program if the data contained an odd number of items?

7.   (a) List the limitations of a **for** loop. (b) What are the advantages of a **while** loop in light
        of your answer to (a)?

8.   What is printed by each of the following programs? (Beware of faulty indentation.)

(a)   ```
        #include <stdio.h>
        void main()
        {
            int i = 1;

            while (i <= 5)
                printf("%d\n", i);
                i++;
        }
        ```

(b)     ```
        #include <stdio.h>
        void main()
        {
            int i = 1;

            while (i <= 5)
            i++;
            printf("%d\n", i);
        }
        ```

9.   Convert the following **for** loop into a **while** loop which has the same effect.

```
count = 0;
sum = 0;
for (i = 1; i <=4; i++) {
        sum = sum + i;
        count++;
}
```

10.   Which of the scanf statements in the following program segment will be executed
        immediately before testing of the condition in the **while** loop header?

```
scanf("%d", &a);
scanf("%d", &b);
while (a > b) {
        scanf("%d  %d", &a, &b);
        scanf("%d  %d", &b, &a);
}
scanf("%d", &c);
```

11.   The following program yields an infinite loop. Diagnose why the problem occurs, and
        state how it can be corrected.

```
#include <stdio.h>
void main()
{
        float x, y;

        x = 4.0;
        y = 1.0;
        while (x != 5) {
                x = x + y / 3;
                printf("%f  %f\n", x, y);
        }
}
```

12. The following faulty program does not process the body of the **while** loop. Diagnose why the problem occurs, and state how it can be corrected.

```
#include <stdio.h>
void main()
{
        int x, y;

        scanf("%d  %d", &x, &y);
        while (x = 0) {
                printf("x is still zero and y is %d\n", y);
                scanf("%d  %d", &x, &y);
        }
}
```

13. What will be printed by the following programs?

(a)
```
#include <stdio.h>
void main()
{
        int w = 8;

        while (w >=2) {
                w = w / 2;
                printf("%d\n", w);
        }
        printf("%d\n", w);
}
```

(b)
```
#include <stdio.h>
void main()
```

```
        {
                int z = 8;

                while (z != 20) {
                        z = z + 6;
                        printf("%d\n", z);
                }
        }
```

(c)   ```
        #include <stdio.h>
        void main()
        {
                int x = 4, count = 0;

                while (x < 50) {
                        x = 2 * x;
                        count++;
                }
                printf("%d %d\n", count, x);
        }
        ```

(d)     ```
        #include <stdio.h>
        void main()
        {
                int y, count;

                y = 17;
                count = 1;
                while (y >=2) {
                        y = y / 3;
                        count = count + 1;
                }
                printf("%d  %d\n", y, count);
        }
        ```

14.   In each of the following program segments, the variable **count** is meant to keep track of the number of data points read until the trailer value is reached (but not including the trailer value). To what value should **count** be initialized before each of the following loops in order for it to reflect the number of data values read? Use the following declarations for each part.

                        int total, count, datum;

(a)   total = 0;   (b)   total = 0;

```
count = ?;                          count = ?;
datum = 0;                          datum = -1;
while (datum != -1000) {            scanf("%d", &datum);
        scanf("%d", &datum);        while (datum != -1000) {
        total = total + datum;              count++;
        count++;                            total = total + datum;
}                                           scanf("%d", &datum);
        ...                         }
                                            ...
```

15.   Write an assignment statement using the variable **count** after each of the following loops
      to accurately reflect the number of data values read (not including the trailer value of
      -1000). Use this declaration for each part:

```
int count, total, datum;
```

   (a)   ```
         count = 0;
         total = 0;
         datum = -1;
         while (datum != -1000) {
                 count++;
                 scanf("%d", datum);
                 total = total + datum;
         }
         ```

   (b)   ```
         count = 0;
         total  = 0;
         datum = -1;
         while (datum != -1000) {
                 scanf("%d", datum);
                 total = total + datum;
                 count++;
         }
         ```

   (c)   ```
         count = 1;
         total = 0;
         datum = -1;
         while (datum != -1000) {
                 count++;
                 scanf("%d", datum);
                 total = total + datum;
         }
         ```

16.   Show exactly what is printed by the following program:
         ```

```
#include <stdio.h>
void main()
{
        int i, j, m;

        j = 1;
        m = 0;
        i = 10;
        while (m <= i) {
                m = 5 * j;
                j++;
                printf("%d\n", m);
        }
        printf("%d  %d  %d\n", i, j, m);
        while (i > 0)
                i = i - 4;
        printf("\n%d  %d  %d\n", i, j, m);
}
```

17.   What will be printed by the following program? Use the data which follow.

```
#include <stdio.h>
void main()
{
        int a, b, c;

        a = -1;
        while (a != -1000) {
                scanf("%d%d%d", &a, &b, &c);
                if (a + b > c) {
                        c = c + 1;
                        a = a + b;
                }
                else    if (a ==b || b == c)
                                a = 1;
                        else {
                                c = 1;
                                b = 1;
                        }
                printf("%d  %d  %d\n", a, b, c);
        }
}
```

```
6    4    9    6    3    9    3    3    5    -1000    0    1
```

18.*   State exactly what will be printed by the following program:

```
#include <stdio.h>
#include <string.h>
void main()
{
        char word[10];
        strcpy(word,"");
        while (strcmp(word, "zzz") != 0) {
                scanf("%s", word);
                printf("%s  %d\n", word, strlen(word));
        }
        printf("%s\n", strcat(word, word));
}
```

data: (Ƅ represents a blank.)
ƄƄƄƄGOOD
ƄƄƄƄƄGOOD
ƄƄƄƄƄƄGOOD
ƄƄƄzzz
zzz

19.*   The program below should read and print an unknown number of names and phone
numbers. At the very end, the number of sets of data should be printed. The program was
run as printed below, and two errors arose:

   •   The phony name and phone number were printed.
   •   The number of real names was over counted by one.

Explain what happened, and show how to correct the program.

```
#include <stdio.h>
#include <string.h>
void main()
{
        int phone, num = 0;
        char name[20];

        strcpy(name, "");
        while (strcmp(name, "zzzzz") != 0) {
                scanf("%s %d", name, &phone);
                printf("%s %d\n", name, phone);
                num++;
        }
        printf("%d sets were read\n", num);
```

```
        }
```

20.* In response to Question 19, a programmer rewrote the program as shown below. Does it work? Explain the advantages and disadvantages of the method used to signal the end of data.

```
#include <stdio.h>
#include <string.h>
void main()
{
        int phone, num = 0;
        char name[20];

        printf("\nEnter a name and a phone number");
        printf("\nEnter a control-z (^Z) when finished.\n");
        while (scanf("%s %d", name, &phone) == 2) {
                printf("%s %d\n", name, phone);
                num++;
        }
        printf("%d sets were read\n", num);
}
```

21. What output is expected from the following program?

```
#include <stdio.h>
void main()
{
        int x, y, z;

        x = 4;
        y = 6;
        z = x - y;
        while (z <= 0) {
                if (x < y)
                        printf("%d  %d  %d\n", x, y, z);
                else {
                        y = y + z;
                        printf("%d  %d\n", y, z);
                }
                printf("%d\n", z);
                x = x + 1;
                z = x - y;
        }
        printf("%d  %d  %d\n", x, y, z);
}
```

22.   What output is expected from the following program?

```
#include <stdio.h>
void main()
{
        int x, y, z;

        x = 3;
        y = -3;
        z = x + y;
        while (x <= 3 && y < 0)              /* see problem 23    */
                if (x <= 3 && y < 0) {       /* for improved style */
                        x = x - 1;
                        y = 2 * x + 4;
                        printf("%d  %d  %d\n", x, y, z);
                }
                else {
                        x = x + 3;
                        z = x + y;
                }
        z = z * z;
        printf("%d  %d  %d\n", x, y, z);
}
```

23.   Criticize the coding within the body of the loop of the last problem.

24.   Criticize the following program. State how it can be improved.

```
#include <stdio.h>
void main()
{
        int count = 1, grade;
        float sum_grades = 0, ave;

        grade = -1;
        scanf("%d", &grade);
        while (grade != -1000) {
                sum_grades = sum_grades + grade;
                count++;
                scanf("%d", &grade);
        }
        ave = sum_grades / count;
}
```

25.   What is printed by the following program?

```
#include <stdio.h>
void main()
{
        int x, y;

        x = 5;
        y = 7;
        if (y > x)
                while (y < 2 * x) {
                        x = x + 1;
                        y = y + 3;
                }
        else
                x = 0;
        printf("%d  %d\n", x, y);
}
```

26.   What will be printed by the following program? Criticize this output.

```
#include <stdio.h>
#include <math.h>
void main()
{
        int i = 0;

        while (i <= 10) {
                i++;
                printf("number   square root   square\n");
                printf("%6d   %11.2f   %6d\n", i, sqrt(i), i * i);
        }
}
```

27.   Write a complete program to do the following: Read an arbitrary (no limit) number of pairs of names — last and first. Print each pair of names as it is read. When all the names have been read, print the number of times the last name "SMITH" occurred, the number of times the first name "JOHN" occurred, and the number of times the names "SMITH" and "JOHN" were read as a pair.

28   Show exactly what is printed by the following program. Use the following data:

```
4    2    5    3
2    4    2    7
```

```
#include <stdio.h>
#define TRUE 1
#define FALSE 0
void main()
{
        int a, w, x, y, z;

        a = TRUE;
        while (a) {
                scanf("%d%d%d%d", &w, &x, &y, &z);
                if (w > x) {
                        x = x + y;
                        y = w + z;
                }
                else   if (x > y) {
                                a = FALSE;
                                w = x + z;
                                y = y + w;
                        }
                printf("%d  %d  %d  %d\n", w, x, y, z);
                if (x == y)
                        if (w < x && y > z)
                                w = 1;
                        else   if (w < z)
                                        x = 1;
                                else y = 1;
                else   if (w + y == z)
                                z = 1;
                printf("%d  %d  %d  %d\n", w, x, y, z);
        }
}
```

29.   What is printed by the following program?

```
#include <stdio.h>
#define TRUE 1
void main()
{
        int i = 1;

        while (TRUE)
                printf("%d\n", i);
}
```

30.   What output is expected from the following program? What is the purpose of the **-1** in the
       input stream?

```
#include <stdio.h>
#define TRUE 1
#define FALSE 0
void main()
{
        int j = TRUE, sum = 0, grade, count = 0;
        char comment1[30], comment2[30], comment3[30];

        while (j) {
                scanf("%d", &grade);
                if (grade < 0)
                        j = FALSE;
                else {
                        sum = sum + grade;
                        count++;
                }
        }
        scanf("%s", comment1);
        scanf("%s", comment2);
        scanf("%s", comment3);
        printf("average  %d\n", sum / count);
        printf("%s  %s  %s\n", comment1, comment2, comment3);
}

data:  82  94  76  99  72  85  -1  EXCELLENT
       GOOD
       POOR
```

31.   Show what will be printed by each of the following programs. Use the data values shown
       below each part.

(a)   ```
#include <stdio.h>
void main()
{
        int i = 0, sum = 0, a = -1;

        scanf("%d", &a);
        while (a != -1000) {
                sum = sum + a;
                i = i + 1;
                scanf("%d", &a);
        }
```
```

```
                    printf("%d  %d\n", sum, i);
        }
```

data: 10   100   20   25   30   35   40   45   -1000

(b)   ```
        #include <stdio.h>
        #define TRUE 1
        #define FALSE 0
        void main()
        {
                int a, i, j;
                float ave, sum;

                j = TRUE;
                i = 0;
                sum = 0;
                while (j) {
                        scanf("%d", &a);
                        sum = sum + a;
                        i++;
                        if (i > 6)
                                j = FALSE;
                }
                printf("%f %d\n", sum, i);
                ave = sum / i;
                printf("%f\n", ave);
        }
        ```

data:   10    100    20    25    30    35    40    45

(c)     ```
        #include <stdio.h>
        #define TRUE 1
        #define FALSE 0
        void main()
        {
                int a, i, j, ave, sum;

                j = TRUE;
                i = 0;
                sum = 0;
                scanf("%d", &a);
                while (j) {
                        sum = sum + a;
                        i++;
                        scanf("%d", &a);
        ```

```
                if (a == 0)
                        j = FALSE;
        }
        printf("%d  %d\n", sum, i);
        ave = sum / i;
        printf("%d\n", ave);
    }
```

data: 10   100   20   25   30   35   40   45   0

32.   What would be the effect of replacing the statement

```
        if (a == 0)
                j = FALSE;
```

in Question 31(c) with each of the following?

(a)   j = a > 0;
(b)   j = a >= 0;
(c)   j = !(a==0);

33.   What is printed by each of the following program segments? Assume that **z** has been declared to be of type **int**. What danger is there in part (a) if **z** is declared to be of type **float**? What is the effect of part (b)?

(a)
```
        z = 2;
        while (z != 20) {
                z = z + 6;
                printf("%d\n", z);
        }
```

(b)
```
        z = 3;
        while (z != 20) {
                z = z + 6;
                printf("%d\n", z);
        }
```

34.   Explain why the second of the following lines might be better than the first to stop a loop when **x** is "equal" to **y**. (Hint: The expression sqrt(4) may be "equal" to 1.9999999.)

```
        float x, y;
```

(a)   **while** (abs(x-y) > 0) **...**
(b)   **while** (abs(x-y) > 1e-6) **...**

Section 4-2   *for* Loops

35.   How many times is HELLO printed in each program?

   (a)   ```
          #include <stdio.h>
          void main()
          {
                  int count;

                  for (count = 1; count <= 7; count++)
                          printf("HELLO\n");
          }
          ```

   (b)    ```
          #include <stdio.h>
          void main()
          {
                  int count;

                  for (count = 87; count <= 93; count++)
                          printf("HELLO\n");
          }
          ```

36.   What is printed by each of the following programs? The data for Part (b) are shown
       below.

   (a)   ```
          #include <stdio.h>
          void main()
          {
                  int count = 0, sum = 0, i;

                  for (i = 1; i <= 4; i++) {
                          sum = sum + i;
                          count = count + 1;
                  }
                  printf("%d %d\n", sum, count);
          }
          ```

   (b)    ```
          #include <stdio.h>
          void main()
          {
                  int count = 0, sum = 0, i, a;

                  for (i = 1; i <= 10; i++) {
                          scanf("%d", &a);
          ```

```
                    count++;
                    sum = sum + a;
              }
              printf("%d  %d  %d\n", sum, count, a);
        }
```

data: 10   20   15   40   5   10   0   9   5   -1

(c)   #include <stdio.h>
        void main()
        {

              int sum, i;

              for (sum = 0, i = 1; i <= 5; sum = sum + i, i++)
                    ;
              printf("sum = %d   i = %d\n", sum, i);
        }

(d)   #include <stdio.h>
        void main()
        {
              int count = 0, sum = 0, i;

              for (i = 4; i >= 1; i--) {
                    count++;
                    sum = sum + count;
              }
              printf("%d %d\n", sum, count);
        }

37.   What is printed by each of the following programs? The only differences between the
      programs are the placement of the initialization statements.

(a)   #include <stdio.h>
        void main()
        {
              int count, sum, i;

              count = 0;
              sum = 0
              for (i = 1; i <= 4; i++) {
                    sum = sum + i;
                    count++;
```
```

```
                }
                printf("%d  %d\n", sum, count);
        }

(b)     #include <stdio.h>
        void main()
        {
                int count, sum, i;

                sum = 0;
                for (i = 1; i <= 4; i++) {
                        count = 0;
                        sum = sum + i;
                        count++;
                }
                printf("%d  %d\n", sum, count);
        }

(c)     #include <stdio.h>
        void main()
        {
                int count, sum, i;

                count = 0;
                for (i = 1; i <= 4; i++) {
                        sum = 0;
                        sum = sum + i;
                        count++;
                }
                printf("%d  %d\n", sum, count);
        }
```

38.   What is printed by the following program:

```
        #include <stdio.h>
        void main()
        {
                int i, n = 0;

                for ( i = 1; i <= n; i++)
                        printf("Garbage\n");
                printf("FINISHED\n");
        }
```

39.   What is printed by each of the following segments? Use the following declaration for each

part.

        int i, j;

(a)   **for** (i = 3; i <= 5; i++)
           printf("%d %d\n", i, i * i);

(b)   **for** (i = 5; i <= 5; i++)
           printf("%d %d\n", i, i * i);

(c)   **for** (i = 3; i < 5; i++)
           printf("%d %d\n", i, i * i);

(d)   **for** (i = 0; i < 5; i++)
           printf("%d %d\n", i, i * i);

(e)   **for** (i = 10; i >= 5; i--)
           printf("%d %d\n", i, i * i);

(f)   j = 5;
      for (i = 10; i <= j; i++)
           printf("%d %d\n", i, i * i);
      printf("%d\n", j);

40.   What is printed by the following program? Use the data shown below.

```
#include <stdio.h>
#include <string.h>
void main()
{
        char a[10], b[10];
        int i, j;

        j = 7;
        for (i = 1; i <=2; i++) {
                scanf("%s%s", a, b);
                if (strlen(a) > strlen(b))
                        printf("A WINNER\n");
                else
                        printf ("B WINNER\n");
                j--;
                scanf("%s%s", a, b);
                if (strlen(a) > strlen(b))
                        printf("A WINNER\n");
                else
```

```
                        printf ("B WINNER\n");
                j--;
        }
        printf("j = %d\n", j);
}
```

```
data:   BOB
        GIBSON
        PHIL
        ESPOSITO
        ABCDE
        IRAN
        TONY
        HEATHER
```

41.   The following segment yielded the value 2 for **j**. Explain.

```
j = 1;
for (i = 1; i <= 10; i++);
        j++;
```

42.   Which of the following initializations is (are) unnecessary and wasteful? Explain why.

```
#include <stdio.h>
void main()
{
        int a, b, c, d, e, f, g, i;

        a = 0;
        b = 0;
        c = 0;
        d = 0;
        e = 0;
        f = 0;
        g = 0;
        i = 0;
        for (i = 1; i <= 10; i++) {
                if (a == b)
                        c = c + 1;
                else
                        d = c + 1;
                e = (b + 1) * (b + 1);
                f = (c + d) / e;
                scanf("%d", &g);
                printf("%d  %d  %d  %d  %d\n", c, d, e, f, g);
```

```
        }
    )
```

43.   What will be printed when the /* *special statement* */ in the following program is
       replaced by each of the following statements?

       (a)   n2 = n2 - 1;
       (b)   i++;
       (c)   n1 = 5;

```
       #include <stdio.h>
       void main()
       {
            int a, n1, n2, i;

            a = 0;
            n1 = 1;
            n2 = 5;
            for (i = n1; i <= n2; i++) {
                 a = 7 * i + a;
                 /* special statement */
                 printf("%d  %d\n", a, n2);
            }
       }
```

44.   How many times is HELLO printed by this program?

```
       #include <stdio.h>
       void main()
       {
            char count;

            for (count = 'a'; count <= 'h'; count++)
                 printf("HELLO\n");
       }
```

Section 4-3   More Complex Loops

45.   How many times is HELLO printed by each of the following programs? Explain the
       difference.

       (a)   #include <stdio.h>
              void main()
              {

```
        int i, j;

        for (i = 1; i <= 3; i++)
                printf("HELLO\n");
        for (j= 1; j <= 4; j++)
                printf("HELLO\n");
}
```

(b)   ```
        #include <stdio.h>
        void main()
        {
                int i, j;

                for (i = 1; i <=3; i++)
                        for (j= 1; j <= 4; j++)
                                printf("HELLO\n");
        }
        ```

46.     What is printed by the following programs?

(a)     ```
        #include <stdio.h>
        void main()
        {
                int i, j, x, y;

                x = 0;
                y = 0;
                for (i = 1; i <= 5; i++) {
                        y++;
                        for ( j = 1; j <= 4; j++)
                                x++;
                }
                printf("%d  %d\n", x, y);
        }
        ```

(b)   ```
        #include <stdio.h>
        void main()
        {
                int i, j, x, y;

                y = 0;
                for (i = 1; i <= 5; i++) {
                        y++;
        ```
        ```

```
                        x = 0;
                        for ( j = 1; j <= 4; j++)
                                x++;
                }
                printf("%d  %d\n", x, y);
        }
```

47.   What are the values of **i** and **j** after execution of each of the following program segments?
       Use this declaration for each part.

```
        int i, j, m, n;
```

(a)
```
        i = 0;
        j = 0;
        for (m = 1; m <= 6; m++) {
                i++;
                for (n = 1; n <= 4; n++)
                        j = j + 4;
        }
```

(b)
```
        i = 0;
        j = 0;
        for (m = 2; m <= 11; m++) {
                i++;
                for (n = 1; n <= 4; n++)
                        j = j + 4;
        }
```

(c)
```
        i = 0;
        j = 0;
        for (m = 1; m <= 6; m++) {
                i++;
                for (n = 14; n >= - 3; n--)
                        j = j + 4;
        }
```

48.   What is printed by the following program?

```
        #include <stdio.h>
        void main()
        {
                int a, i;

                a = 1;
                i = 2;
```

```
                    while (a < 23 && i < 11) {
                            i = i + 1;
                            a = 2 * a;
                    }
                    printf("%d  %d\n", i, a);
            }
```

49.   (a) What is printed by the following program?

```
            #include <stdio.h>
            void main()
            {
                    int k, m;

                    k = 10;;
                    m = -1000;
                    while (m < 30 && k < 20) {
                            m = k * 2;
                            printf("%d  %d\n", k, m);
                            m = k / 2;
                            k = k + 1;
                    }
                    printf("%d  %d\n", k, m);
            }
```

(b) Would the result be any different if the condition in the **while** loop were reversed (i.e., **k < 20 && m < 30**). Why or why not?

50.   What will be printed by the following program?

```
            #include <stdio.h>
            void main()
            {
                    int r, x;

                    x = 6;
                    r = 1;
                    while (x > 0 && r <= 10) {
                            x = 1 + 4 * r - r * r;
                            printf("%d  %d\n", r, x);
                            r++;
                    }
            }
```

51.   What is printed by the following program?

```
#include <stdio.h>
void main()
{
        int a, i;

        a = 0;
        i = 2;
        while (a < 9 && i <= 13) {
                a = a + 2;
                i = i + 3;
        }
        printf("%d  %d\n", i, a);
}
```

52.   What is printed by the following program?

```
#include <stdio.h>
void main()
{
        int i, j;

        for ( i = 1; i <= 5; i++) {
                j = 5;
                while ( i != j && j >= 1) {
                        printf("%d  %d\n", i, j);
                        j--;
                }
                printf("%d  %d\n", i, j);
        }
}
```

Section 4-4 *do-while* Loops

53.   What are the differences between a **while** loop and a **do - while** loop?

54.   Which type of loop (**while** or **do - while**) normally has some type of initialization before
       the loop? Why?

55.   Convert the following **while** loop into a **do - while** loop:

```
scanf("%d", &a);
while (a != -1000) {
        sum = sum + a;
```

```
        i = i + 1;
        scanf("%d", &a);
    }
```

56. Translate the flowchart in Figure 4-1 into C code.

Figure 4-1   Flowchart for Translation to C

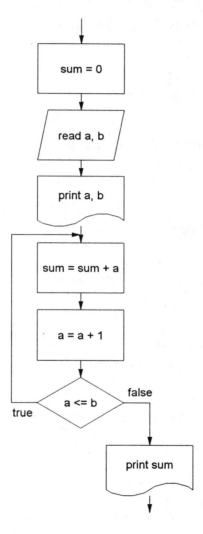

57. Convert the following **while** loop into a **do-while** loop. Assume that the body of the loop will be done at least once.

```
        while (a > b) {
            /* body of loop */
        }
```

58.   Convert the following **while** loop into a **do-while** loop. Assume that the body of the
       loop will be done at least once.

```
while (a > b && a == d) {
        /* body of loop */
}
```

59.   Convert the following **while** loop into a **do-while** loop. Assume that the body of the
       loop will be done at least once.

```
while (a > b || a > d) {
        /* body of loop */
}
```

60.   Convert the following **while** loop into a **do-while** loop.

```
i = 1;
while ( i <= 5) {
        scanf("%d", &i);
        /* body of loop */
}
```

61.   Convert the following **while** loop into a **do-while** loop.

```
scanf("%d", &x);
while ( x != 5) {
        /* body of loop */
        scanf("%d", &x);
}
```

62.   Convert the following **do-while** loop into a **while** loop.

```
scanf("%d", &x);
do
        /* body of loop */
        scanf("%d", &x);
while (x !=5);
```

63.   Convert the following **while** loop into a **do-while** loop.

```
scanf("%d", &x);
while ( !(abs(x) < 3)) {
        /* body of loop */
        scanf("%d", &x);
```

```
        }
```

Section 4-5 *break* and *continue* statements

64.   What is printed by each of the following programs. For each program use the data shown
        below. (Note: Some of the data given may not be used.)

                data: 10   20   15   40   5   10   0   9   5   -1   6   -100

(a)   ```
        #include <stdio.h>
        void main()
        {
                int count = 0, sum = 0, i, a;

                for (i = 1; i <= 10; i++) {
                        scanf("%d", &a);
                        count++;
                        if (count == 5)
                                break;
                        sum = sum + a;
                }
                printf("%d %d %d\n", sum, count, a);
        }
        ```

(b)     ```
        #include <stdio.h>
        void main()
        {
                int count = 0, sum = 0, i, a;

                for (i = 1; i <= 10; i++) {
                        scanf("%d", &a);
                        count++;
                        if (a == 15)
                                continue;
                        sum = sum + a;
                }
                printf("%d  %d  %d\n", sum, count, a);
        }
        ```

(c)   ```
        #include <stdio.h>
        void main()
        {
        ```
        ```

```
        int count = 0, sum = 0, i, a;

        for (i = 1; i <= 10; i++) {
                scanf("%d", &a);
                count++;
                if (a == 15)
                        break;
                sum = sum + a;
        }
        printf("%d  %d  %d\n", sum, count, a);
}
```

(d)   #include <stdio.h>
        void main()
        {
```
                int count = 0, sum = 0, i, a;

                for (i = 1; i <= 10; i++) {
                        scanf("%d", &a);
                        count++;
                        if (count == 5)
                                continue;
                        sum = sum + a;
                }
                printf("%d  %d  %d\n", sum, count, a);
        }
```

65.   What will be printed by the following program? Use the data which follows:

```
        #include <stdio.h>
        #define TRUE 1
        void main()
        {
                int a, b, c;

                a = -1;
                while (TRUE) {
                        scanf("%d%d%d", &a, &b, &c);
                        if (a == -1000)
                                break;
                        if (a + b > c) {
                                c = c + 1;
                                a = a + b;
                        }
```

```
                else    if (a ==b || b == c)
                                a = 1;
                        else {
                                c = 1;
                                b = 1;
                        }
                printf("%d  %d  %d\n", a, b, c);
        }
}
```

6   4   9   6   3   9   3   3   5   -1000   0   1

66.   What is printed by the following programs?

(a)   ```
       #include <stdio.h>
       void main()
       {
               int i, j, x, y;

               x = 0;
               y = 0;
               for (i = 1; i <= 5; i++) {
                       y++;
                       for (j = 1; j <= 4; j++) {
                               if (x == 4)
                                       continue;
                               x++;
                       }
               }
               printf("%d %d\n", x, y);
       }
       ```

(b)    ```
       #include <stdio.h>
       void main()
       {
               int i, j, x, y;

               x = 0;
               y = 0;
               for (i = 1; i <= 5; i++) {
                       y++;
                       for ( j = 1; j <= 4; j++) {
                               if (x == 4)
                                       break;
                               x++;
       ```

```
                }
        }
        printf("%d  %d\n", x, y);
}
```

(c)   ```
        #include <stdio.h>
        void main()
        {
                int i, j, x, y;

                x = 0;
                y = 0;
                for (i = 1; i <= 5; i++) {
                        y++;
                        if (x == 4)
                                continue;
                        for (j = 1; j <= 4; j++)
                                x++;
                }
                printf("%d %d\n", x, y);
        }
        ```

(d)     ```
        #include <stdio.h>
        void main()
        {
                int i, j, x, y;

                x = 0;
                y = 0;
                for (i = 1; i <= 5; i++) {
                        y++;
                        if (x == 4)
                                break;
                        for ( j = 1; j <= 4; j++)
                                x++;
                }
                printf("%d  %d\n", x, y);
        }
        ```

Section 4-6 *switch* statements

67.   (a) Show what is printed by the following program. Use the data given below.

        A   B   B   F   C

```
#include <stdio.h>
void main()
{
        char grade;

        while (scanf("%c", &grade) == 1)
                switch(grade) {
                        case 'A':       printf("Exceptional\n");
                                        break;
                        case 'B':
                        case 'C':       printf("OK\n");
                                        break;
                        case 'D':       printf("COULD DO BETTER\n");
                                        break;
                        case 'F':       printf("FAILING\n");
                }
}
```

(b) What would happen if the **break** statements shown above were omitted? Why is there no **break** statement after the last case?

68.*   Show what is printed by the following program? Assume the following set of data:

        3   0   6   11   9   4   12   8   2

```
#include <stdio.h>
void main()
{
        int month, period;
        void season(int);
        int printmonth(int);

        while (scanf("%d", &month) == 1) {
                if (month == 8)
                        break;
                period = printmonth(month);
                season(period);
        }
}

int printmonth(int month)
{
        char * word[12] =
```

```
                              {"Jan", "Feb", "Mar", "Apr", "May", "Jun", "Jul", "Aug",
                                   "Sep", "Oct", "Nov", "Dec"};
            int season;
            if (month >=1 && month <=12)
                    printf("%s  ", word[month-1]);
            else
                    printf("Err  ");
            if (month == 1 || month == 2 || month == 12)
                    season = 1;
            else if (month >= 3 && month <= 5)
                    season = 2;
            else if (month >= 6 && month <=8)
                    season = 3;
            else if (month >= 9  && month <=11)
                    season = 4;
            else
                    season = 0;
            return season;
    }


    void season(int period)
    {
            switch (period) {
                    case 1:        printf(" winter\n");    break;
                    case 2:        printf(" spring\n");    break;
                    case 3:        printf(" summer\n");  break;
                    case 4:        printf(" fall\n");        break;
                    default:      printf(" error\n");
            }
    }
```

69.   Show what is printed by the following program. Assume that the user inputs the characters **befa** followed by a control-Z (^Z). Note: the ASCII value of **'a'** is 97.

```
        #include <stdio.h>
        void main()
        {
            int c, let;

            while (scanf("%c", &c) == 1) {
                    switch (c) {
                            case 'a' :     let = c + 1;    break;
                            case 'b':
                            case 'd':      let = c - 1;    break;
                            case 'e':      let = 'b';      break;
```

```
                     default:        let = 'x';
            }
            printf("%c  %c  %d\n", c, let, c);
        }
    }
```

CHAPTER 5 - TURBO C INPUT/OUTPUT

Section 5-1 Writing to the Screen (*stdout*)

1.   What is printed by the following program segment?

```
char word[10];

strcpy(word, "Hello  \n");
printf("word is  %s",  word);
```

2.   What will be printed by the following program segment? Assume the variables are declared to have data type **int**.

```
number1 = 123;
number2 = 456;
printf("%d%d\n",number1, number2);
printf("%d\n%d",number1, number2);
```

3.   Which of the following calls to the **printf** function would cause the most consecutive blank spaces to be placed in the output?

(a)   printf("%s%s\n", "THE",   "END");

(b)   printf("%s   %s\n", "THE", "END");

(c)   printf("%s%s%s\n",
            "WHEN YOU HAVE A LONG STRING TO OUTPUT ",
            "IT CAN DETRACT FROM THE INDENTATION PATTERN OF ",
            "YOUR PROGRAM");

(d)   printf("%s%s%s%s%s%s\n",
            "IF YOU PUT YOUR STRINGS ",
            "INTO SEVERAL STRING ",
            "CONSTANTS, YOU CAN MINIMIZE ",
            "THE NUMBER OF BLANKS ",
            "AND STILL KEEP YOUR ",
            "INDENTATION PATTERN");

4.   Assume that each of the following numbers represents a value for the variable **x**, which has been declared to be of type **float**. Give a call to the **printf** function which will print each in standard decimal form, with at least one digit to the left of the decimal point. Use the smallest field width possible and allow no more decimal places than necessary. Show how each number prints.

(a) 1.3689400050e+01
(b) 3.2100000000e-03
(c) 6.0562000000e+00
(d) -0.3923046875e+02
(e) 0.8860000000e-01

5.   (a) What format specification would you use in the **printf** function to print **x**, a real number, in scientific notation?
(b) To print in decimal notation, how can you specify the field width and the number of decimal places?
(c) How can you specify the number of decimal places in decimal notation, but not the field width?

6.   What is the purpose of the **#include <stdio.h>** preprocessor directive?

7.   What will be printed by the following program?

```
#include <stdio.h>
#define TRUE 1
void main()
{
        int x = 1, flag = TRUE;

        printf("%d %d", x, flag);
}
```

8.   What will be printed by the following program segment? Assume all variables are declared to be of type **float**.

```
number1 = 1.2300e+01;
number2 = 5.67;
printf("%4.1f\n", number1);
printf("%5.1f\n", number1);
printf("%5.2f\n", number1);
printf("%4.2f\n", number2);
printf("%3.1f\n", number2);
printf("%5.1f\n", number2);
```

9.   What will be printed by the following program segment?

```
char    vara[10] = "mickey",
        varb[10] = "mouse",
        varc[10] = "donald",
        vard[10] = "duck";
```

```
printf("%s%7s%9s%s\n", vara, varb, varc, vard);
printf("%8s\n", vara);
printf("%8s\n", varb);
printf("%8s\n", varc);
printf("%8s\n", vard);
```

10.   (a) Neatly tabulate, without using a computer, the following "contributions to the Boston Tea Party."

Adam, John	10.00	Burrr, Aaron	1.98
Franklin, Benjamin	20.00	Washington, George	100.00

(b) Explain how to get the alphabetic data left justified (starting in the first column in a field) and numeric data right justified (ending in the last column in a field).

(c) Show what your table from Part (a) would look like if alphabetic data were printed right justified and numeric data were printed left justified.

11.   What will be printed by the following program segment? Assume all variables are declared to be of type **int**.

```
number1 = 12345;
number2 = 9876;
printf("%d\n", number1);
printf("%d", number2);
printf("%d", number1);
```

12.   What will be printed by the following program segment?

```
char    variable1[10] = "my",
        variable2[10] = "gosh";

printf("oh%s%s\n", variable1, variable2);
printf("oh %s %s\n", variable1,variable2);
printf("%s %s %s\n", "oh", variable1, variable2);
```

13.   What will be printed by the following program segment?

```
char    variable1[10] = "quail  ",
        variable2[10] = "quaint  ",
        variable3[10] = "quake  ";

printf("%s", variable1);
```

```
printf("%s", variable2);
printf("%s\n", variable3);
printf("Will this be printed on a new line?");
printf("  I think so.\n");
```

14.   What will be printed by the following program?

```
#include <stdio.h>
#include <string.h>
void main()
{
        int a, b;
        float c, d;
        char str1[10], str2[10];

        a = 1;
        b = 2;
        c = 3;
        d = 4;
        strcpy(str1, "one");
        strcpy(str2, "two");
        printf("%d", a);
        printf("%d\n", b);
        printf("%f", c);
        printf("%f", d);
        printf("%s%s\n", str1, str2);
        printf("%s%d%d", str2, a, b);
}
```

15.   What will be printed by the following program segment? Assume that **number** has been declared to be of type **float**.

```
number = 16;
printf("%f%f\n", number, 0.314);
```

16.   What is printed by the following program?

```
#include <stdio.h>
void main()
{
        float x = 1234.4329;

        printf("x = %f\n", x);
        printf("-x = %f\n", -x);
```

```
            printf("x = %8f\n", x);
            printf("x = %9.4f\n", x);
            printf("x = %7.3f\n", x);
            printf("x = %8.3f\n", x);
            printf("x = %10.3f\n", x);
        }
```

17.   Show how to print a variable, named **str**, which represents a string of up to 80 characters
       (i.e., declared **char str[80];**), centered on an 80-column page, no matter what its length.

Section 5-2   Read Interactively from the Keyboard (*stdin*)

18.   Suppose we have the following declarations:

               char name[15];
               float num;

       (a) Using these variables, write the C statement(s) to read "Joe" into **name** (with no
       blanks) and 4.5 into **num**.

       (b) Using these variables, write the C statement(s) to print these lines:

           Joe
             4.50

19.   What will happen upon execution of the following program, using the following data:

           34<cr>   5.6<cr>   (<cr> means carriage return.)

           #include <stdio.h>
           void main()
           {
                   float floatno;
                   int intno;

                   scanf("%f", &floatno);
                   scanf("%d", &intno);
                   printf("%f\n", floatno);
                   printf("%d\n", intno);
           }

20.   What will be the values of the various variables at the end of this program segment?
       Assume that the variables have been declared to be of type **int**. (<cr> means carriage
       return.)

```
scanf("%d", &number1);
scanf("%d", &number2);
scanf("%d", &number3);
```

(a)   123<cr>
        456   789<cr>
        321   654<cr>

(b)   123   456   789   321   654<cr>

(c)   123<cr>
        456<cr>
        <cr>
        789 <cr>
        321   654<cr>

21.   What is whitespace, and how does it effect the **%s** format specifier when used in a **scanf** function?

22.   What is the purpose of the **&** operator when used in the **scanf** function, and why is it *not* used when reading strings?

23.   What will be the values of **str** and **num** in the following program segments? Assume the following declarations:

```
char str[8];
int num;
```

(a)   scanf("%s%d", str, &num);

column	1	9
	delta	88<cr>

(b)   scanf("%s%d", str, &num);

column	1	5	13
		delta	88<cr>

(c)   scanf("%d%s", &num, str);

column	1	4
	88	delta<cr>

(d)   scanf("%d%s", &num, str);

```
column     1        9
           88       delta<cr>
```

Section 5-3 Read from an External file (*fscanf*)

24.   Complete the statements below so that the values of **x** and **y** are read from an external file
      called *test.dat* which is stored on a diskette which has been placed in drive *a:*.

```c
#include <stdio.h>
void main()
{
        int x, y;
        FILE * ?????;

        datafile = fopen("?????", "?????");

        fscanf(?????, "%d %d", &x, &y);
        printf("%d  %d", x, y);

        fclose(?????);
}
```

25.   Show exactly what will be printed by the following program. The external file on disk
      contains three lines:

```
1
2
3
```

      (Note: The square root of 2 is 1.4142135, and the square root of 3 is 1.7320508.)

```c
#include <stdio.h>
#include <math.h>
void main()
{
        int x, y;
        float z;
        FILE * datafile;

        datafile = fopen("a:extname.dat", "r");

        while (fscanf(datafile, "%d", &x) == 1) {
                y = x * x * x - x * x + x / 2;
```

```
                            z = sqrt(x);
                            printf("x = %d    y = %d    z = %f\n", x, y, z);
               }

                    fclose(datafile);
      }
```

26. What will be the values of **str** and **num** in the following program segments? Values will be read from an external file (non-interactive). Compare these results with those of Exercise 23. Assume the following declarations:

```
      char str[8];
      int num;
```

(a)   fscanf(infile, "%s%d", str, &num);

column	1	9
	delta	88<cr>

(b)   fscanf(infile, "%s%d", str, &num);

column	1	5	13
		delta	88<cr>

(c)   fscanf(infile, "%d%s", &num, str);

column	1	4
	88	delta<cr>

(d)   fscanf("%d%s", &num, str);

column	1	9	20
	88	delta	<cr>

27. Prepare a data file named *input.dat* on disk. Place a digit on each of the first four lines. Do not put a carriage return on the fourth line. Run the following program. Then edit the data file by putting a carriage return on the fourth line. Rerun the program, and see what difference the carriage return makes, if any. Again edit the data file by putting a carriage return (only) on the fifth line, and again rerun the program. What did you learn about carriage returns at the end of data files?

```
            #include <stdio.h>
            void main()
            {
                    int x;
```

```
                        FILE * datafile;

                        datafile = fopen("a:input.dat", "r");

                        printf("begun\n");
                        while (fscanf(datafile, "%d", &x) == 1) {
                                printf("in loop\n");
                                printf("x = %d\n", x);
                        }

                        fclose(datafile);
                }
```

28.   Repeat the experiment of Exercise 27, using the following program. Explain the reason
       why the results are different.

```
                #include <stdio.h>
                void main()
                {
                        int x;
                        FILE * datafile;

                        datafile = fopen("a:input.dat", "r");

                        printf("begun\n");
                        while (!feof(datafile)) {
                                fscanf(datafile, "%d", &x);
                                printf("in loop\n");
                                printf("x = %d\n", x);
                        }

                        fclose(datafile);
                }
```

Section 5-4   Writing to an External file (*fprintf*)

29.   Complete the statements below so that a file called *results.prt* is created on drive *a*: which
       contains a table of squares, square roots and cubes of the numbers 1 to 10.

```
                #include <stdio.h>
                #include <math.h>
                void main()
                {
```

```
int x;
FILE * ?????;

results = fopen("?????", "?????");

fprintf(results, "Number     Square Root      Cube\n");
for (x = 1; x <= 10; x++)
        fprintf(results, "%6d%14.2f%14d\n", x, sqrt(x), x * x * x);

fclose(?????);
}
```

30.   What changes would you make to your answer in Exercise 29, so that the results would be printed directly to the printer?

31.   What is the difference between the **w** and the **w+** file mode string?

32.   Write a C program that will read a datafile, *input.dat*, containing an unknown number of lines each containing a last name and first name followed by three integers representing the student's grades; and is to create an output file, *output.dat*, containing the students name and average. For example, if the input.dat file contained the lines:

```
She, Ms.          80   75   80
Someone, Joe      90   90   90
Smith, Sally      99   90   85
```

then, the *output.out* file would contain the lines:

```
She, Ms.          78
Someone, Joe      90
Smith, Sally      91
```

33.   Assume you have prepared a datafile, *names.dat* which contains an unknown number of lines each containing a last name and first name followed by the integer 0 if the individual is a male or 1 if the individual is female. Write a C program that reads the names from the *names.dat* file and places them into a file called *men.out* or *women.out* based upon their gender.

Section 5-5   Testing for End-of-File

34.   In each of the following program segments, the variable **count** is meant to keep track of the number of data points read. To what value should **count** be initialized before each of the following loops in order for it to reflect the number of data values read until the end-of-file condition is raised?

```
int total, count, datum;
FILE * infile;
```

(a)
```
total = 0;
count = ?;
fscanf(infile, "%d", &datum);
while (!feof(infile)) {
        total = total + datum;
        count++;
        fscanf(infile, "%d", &datum);
}
```

(b)
```
total = 0;
count = ?;
fscanf(infile, "%d", &datum);
while (!feof(infile)) {
        count++;
        total = total + datum;
        fscanf(infile, "%d", &datum);
}
```

(c)
```
total = 0;
count = ?;
while (fscanf(infile, "%d", &datum) == 1) {
        count++;
        total = total + datum;
}
```

35.   Complete the statement after each of the following loops to accurately reflect the number of data values read. Use the following declarations for each part.

```
int count, total, datum, number_of_data;
FILE * infile;
```

(a)
```
count = 0;
total = 0;
fscanf(infile, "%d", &datum);
while (!feof(infile)) {
        count++;
        total = total + datum;
        fscanf(infile, "%d", &datum);
}
number_of_data = ?;
```

(b)
```
count = 0;
total = 0;
fscanf(infile, "%d", &datum);
while (!feof(infile)) {
        total = total + datum;
        count++;
        fscanf(infile, "%d", &datum);
}
number_of_data = ?;
```

(c)
```
count = 1;
total = 0;
fscanf(infile, "%d", &datum);
while (!feof(infile)) {
        count++;
        total = total + datum;
        fscanf(infile, "%d", &datum);
}
number_of_data = ?;
```

(d)
```
count = 0;
total = 0;
while (fscanf(infile, "%d", &datum) == 1) {
        count++;
        total = total + datum;
}
number_of_data = ?;
```

(e)
```
count = 1;
total = 0;
while (fscanf(infile, "%d", &datum) == 1) {
        count++;
        total = total + datum;
}
number_of_data = ?;
```

36. What will be printed by each of the following C programs, using the set of data which follows? Explain the reason for the different results.

    6   4   9   6 3 9   3 3 5   353

(a)
```
#include <stdio.h>
void main()
{
```

```
            int a, b, c;
            FILE * infile;

            infile = fopen("a:input.dat", "r");
            fscanf(infile, "%d%d%d", &a, &b, &c);
            while (!feof(infile)) {
                    if (a + b > c) {
                            c = c + 1;
                            a = a + b;
                    }
                    else    if (a == b || b == c)
                                    a = 1;
                            else {
                                    c = 1;
                                    b = 1;
                            }
                    printf("%d   %d   %d\n", a, b, c);
                    fscanf(infile, "%d%d%d", &a, &b, &c);
            }
            fclose(infile);
    }

(b)     #include <stdio.h>
        void main()
        {
            int a, b, c;
            FILE * infile;

            infile = fopen("a:input.dat", "r");
            while (!feof(infile)) {
                    fscanf(infile, "%d%d%d", &a, &b, &c);
                    if (a + b > c) {
                            c = c + 1;
                            a = a + b;
                    }
                    else    if (a == b || b == c)
                                    a = 1;
                            else {
                                    c = 1;
                                    b = 1;
                            }
                    printf("%d   %d   %d\n", a, b, c);
            }
            fclose(infile);
        }
```

37.   State exactly what will be printed by each of the following programs. Use the data below.

```
data:   GOOD
          GOOD
              GOOD
        MORNING
```

(a)
```
#include <stdio.h>
#include <string.h>
void main()
{
        char word[10];
        FILE * infile;

        infile = fopen("a:input.dat", "r");
        while (fscanf(infile, "%s", word) == 1)
                printf("%s   %d\n", word, strlen(word));
        printf("%s%s\n", word, word);
        fclose(infile);
}
```

(b)
```
#include <stdio.h>
#include <string.h>
void main()
{
        char word[10];
        FILE * infile;

        infile = fopen("a:input.dat", "r");
        fscanf(infile, "%s", word);
        while (!feof(infile)) {
                printf("%s   %d\n", word, strlen(word));
                fscanf(infile, "%s", word);
        }
        printf("%s%s\n", word, word);
        fclose(infile);
}
```

38.   The program below should read and print an unknown number of names and phone numbers. At the very end, the number of lines of data should be printed. A datafile was prepared and the program was run as printed below, and two errors arose:

   •   The last name and phone number on the list were printed twice.

- The number of names was over counted by one.

Explain what happened, and show how to correct the program.

```
#include <stdio.h>
void main()
{
        int num, phone;
        char name[20];
        FILE * infile;

        infile = fopen("a:input.dat", "r");
        num = 0;
        while (!feof(infile)) {
                fscanf(infile, "%s%d", name, &phone);
                printf("%s   %d\n", name, phone);
                num++;
        }
        printf("%d lines were read\n", num);
        fclose(infile);
}
```

39.   Criticize the following program. State how it can be improved. What error, if any, may occur?

```
#include <stdio.h>
void main()
{
        int  count = 1, grade;
        float sum_grade = 0.0, ave;
        FILE * infile;

        infile = fopen("a:input.dat", "r");
        while (!feof(infile)) {
                fscanf(infile, "%d", &grade);
                sum_grade = sum_grade + grade;
                count++;
        }
        ave = sum_grade / count;
        printf("average = %f\n", ave);
}
```

40.   Show what will be printed by the following program.

```
#include <stdio.h>
```

```
void main()
{
        int i = 0, sum = 0, a;
        FILE * infile;

        infile = fopen("a:input.dat", "r");
        while (fscanf(infile, "%d", &a) == 1) {
                sum = sum + a;
                i++;
        }
        printf("%d  %d  %d\n", sum, i, a);
        fclose(infile);
}
```

data: 10   100   20   25   30   35   40   45

41.   What values are printed by the following program?

```
#include <stdio.h>
#include <string.h>
void main()
{
        char a[20], b[20];
        int j = 0;
        FILE * infile;

        infile = fopen("a:input.dat", "r");
        while (fscanf(infile, "%s%s", a, b) == 2) {
                if (strlen(a) > strlen(b))
                        printf("A WINNER\n");
                else
                        printf("B WINNER\n");
                j++;
        }
        printf("j = %d\n", j);
        fclose(infile);
}
```

data: MEM1
           MEM2
         DROOL12345678
         SPOCK

CHAPTER 6 - INTEGER AND CHARACTER VARIABLES

1. Evaluate each of the following, assuming that each variable has been declared to be of type **int**:

    (a) a = (3 + 4) / 2;
    (b) b = 3 + 5 % 2 + 7 * (5 -1);
    (c) c = 2 + 3 * 5 / 2 + 3 % 3 * (5 - 4);

2. What will be printed by the following program?

    ```
    #include <stdio.h>
    void main()
    {
            int a = 1, b = 2, c = 3;
            float x, y;

            c = c + a++;
            b = c + b / c;
            x = (a + 3) / 2;
            y = (x + 3) * c / 3.0;
            printf("a = %d    b = %d    c = %d\n", a, b, c);
            printf("x = %f    y = %f\n", x, y);

    }
    ```

3. (a) What is the largest integer that can be stored in two bytes? four bytes?
    (b) What is the largest integer that can be represented on the machine which you are using?

4. What is the cause of the unexpected answer produced by the following program and how may it be avoided?

    ```
    #include <stdio.h>
    void main()
    {
            int a, b;

            a = 15000;
            b = a  * 3;
            printf("%d   %d\n", a, b);
    }
    ```

5. What is printed by the following program?

```
#include <stdio.h>
#include <math.h>
void main()
{
        int a, b, c, d, e;

        a = 2;
        b = 3;

        c = abs(5 * (a - b) + 1);
        d = pow(a, b);
        e = pow(2, 5) + pow(2, 6);
        printf("%d  %d  %d  %d  %d\n", a, b, c, d, e);
}
```

6.   What does the following program produce:

```
#include <stdio.h>
#include <math.h>
void main()
{
        int i , j;

        for (i = 1; i <= 5; i++)
              for (j = 1; j <= 5; j ++)
                    printf("%5d%5.0f%5.0f\n", i * j, pow(i, j), pow (j, i));
}
```

7.   What would be the result of the program in Exercise 6 if the conversion character used in the **printf** function would be **%d** rather than **%f**?

8.   What is the result of the following program? (Note: The ASCII value of 'a' is 97.)

```
#include <stdio.h>
void main()
{
        int i;
        char c;

        c = 'a';
        for (i = 1; i <=5; i++)
              printf("%d   %c    %d\n", i, c + i, c + i);
}
```

9.   How many bytes are used to store a variable whose type is **char**?

10.   What is the largest *integer* that can be stored in a variable whose type has been declared
       to be of type **char**?

11.   Indicate the expected result of the following program?

```
#include <stdio.h>
void main()
{
        int c;

        while ((c = getchar()) != EOF) {
                putchar(c);
                putchar(c);
        }
}
```

12.   In Exercise 11, why is **c** declared to be of type **int** rather than of type **char**?

13.   (a) Suppose the program in Exercise 11 was saved on disk *a:* under the name *double.c*
       and a text file known as *infile.dat* was also created on disk *a:*, using redirection, what
       would be typed at the DOS C> prompt so that *infile.dat* could be processed by *double.c*?

       (b) Without rewriting the program in Exercise 11, show what would be typed at the C>
       prompt so that the results would be redirected to the printer.

14.   What is the result of the following program, using the data given below:

```
data:   aAaa bbC
        cc

#include <stdio.h>
void main()
{
        int i = 0, c;

        while ((c = getchar()) != EOF)
                if (c >='a' && c <= 'z'){
                        putchar(c);
                        i++;
                }
        printf("%d\n", i);
}
```

15. Using the data shown below, what will be printed by the following program?

```
data:   The Cat In The
        Hat
        And
        The Cat in the Hat
        Comes Back
        1 Cat, 2 Cats, 3 Cats
```

```c
#include <stdio.h>
void main()
{
        int i = 0, c;

        while ((c = getchar()) != EOF) {
                if (c == '\n')
                        putchar('\n');
                putchar(c);
        }
}
```

16. Using the data given in Exercise 15, what will be the result of the following program?

```c
#include <stdio.h>
void main()
{
        int i = 0, c;

        while ((c = getchar()) != EOF)
                if (c >='a' && c < 'z'){
                        putchar(c + 'A' - 'a');
                        i++;
                }
                else
                        putchar(c);
        printf("%d\n", i);
}
```

17. Using the data given in Exercise 15, what will be the result to the following program?

```c
#include <stdio.h>
#include <ctype.h>
void main()
{
```

```
            int lower = 0, upper = 0, digits = 0, i = 0, c;

            while ((c = getchar()) != EOF) {
                if (isalpha(c))
                        if (islower(c)) {
                                lower++;
                                c = toupper(c);
                        }
                        else {
                                upper++;
                                c = tolower(c);
                        }
                else   if (isdigit(c))
                                digits++;
                putchar(c);
                i++;
            }
            printf("%d   %d   %d   %d\n", i, lower, upper, digits);
        }
```

18.   Consulting the ASCII Chart in Table 6-1, what will be printed by the following program?

```
        #include <stdio.h>
        void main()
        {
            int i, j;
            char c, d;

            i = 'Z';
            j = i - 5;
            c = 110;
            d = c - 'Y' + 30;
            printf("Numbers:    %d   %d   %d   %d\n", i, j, c, d);
            printf("Characters: %c    %c    %c    %c\n", i, j, c, d);
        }
```

Table 6-1   ASCII Values

American Standard Code for Information Interchange

Left/Right Digits	0	1	2	3	4	5	6	7	8	9
0	nul	so	stx	etx	eot	en	ac	bel	bs	ht
1	nl	vt	np	cr	so	si	dle	dcl	dc2	dc3
2	dc	na	sy	etb	can	em	su	es	fs	gs
3	rs	us	sp	!	"	#	$	%	&	'
4	(	)	*	+	`	-	.	/	0	1
5	2	3	4	5	6	7	8	9	:	;
6	<	=	>	?	@	A	B	C	D	E
7	F	G	H	I	J	K	L	M	N	O
8	P	Q	R	S	T	U	V	W	X	Y
9	Z	[	\	]	^	_	,	a	b	c
10	d	e	f	g	h	i	j	k	l	m
11	n	o	p	q	r	s	t	u	v	w
12	x	y	z	{	|	}	~	del		

Notes:
1.   Character codes 0-31 and 127 are nonprinting.
2.   Some abbreviations:

bel	audible bell
bs	backspace
cr	carriage return
esc	escape
ht	horizontal tab
nl	newline
nul	null
sp	single space
vt	vertical tab

Chapter 7 - Functions

Section 7-1   Functions

1.   Show what is printed by the following program consisting of two functions **main** and **compare**. Use the following data:

```
-14   1     6   2       5   4
```

```c
#include <stdio.h>
void main()
{
        int i, x, y, z;
        int compare(int, int);

        for (i = 1; i <= 3; i++) {
                scanf("%d%d", &x, &y);
                z = compare(x, y);
                printf("%d   %d   %d\n", x, y, z);
        }
}

int compare(int a, int b)
{
        if (a > b + 2)
                return a + b;
        else
                return a - b;
}
```

2.   Show what is printed by the following program consisting of two functions. Use the following data:

```
-14   1     6   2       5   4       0   0
```

```c
#include <stdio.h>
#define TRUE 1
#define FALSE 0
void main()
{
        int x, y, is_x_bigger;
        int compare(int a, int b);

        scanf("%d%d", &x, &y);
```

```
                    while (x != 0 || y !=0) {
                            is_x_bigger = compare(x, y);
                            if (is_x_bigger)
                                    printf(" x is bigger\n");
                            else
                                    printf(" y is bigger\n");
                            scanf("%d%d", &x, &y);
                    }
            }

            int compare(int a, int b)
            {
                    if (a > b + 2)
                            return TRUE;
                    else
                            return FALSE;
            }
```

3.   Show what is printed by the following program consisting of two functions. The following
     data is in an external file, *infile.dat*, which is made available to the program using input
     redirection:

```
-14    1     6   2        5   4  <cr>              (<cr> means carriage return)
```

```
#include <stdio.h>
void main()
{
        int x, y, is_x_bigger;
        char * message;
        char * compare(int a, int b);

        while (scanf("%d%d", &x, &y) == 2) {
                message = compare(x, y);
                printf("%d   %d   %s\n", x, y, message);
        }
}

char * compare(int a, int b)
{
        if (a > b + 2)
                return "first is bigger";
        else
                return "second is bigger";
}
```

4.   Write a function **cuberoot** which accepts as an argument a **float** number and returns the cube root of the number. Why do you think that **cuberoot** isn't in the **math.h** portion of the standard library?

5.   Show exactly what is printed by the following program:

```
#include <stdio.h>
void main()
{
        int a, b, c;
        int multiply(int, int);

        a = 2;
        b = 4;
        c = multiply(a, b);
        printf("%d   %d   %d\n", a, b, c);
        b = multiply(b, a);
        printf("%d   %d   %d\n", a, b, c);
        a = multiply(a, a);
        printf("%d   %d   %d\n", a, b, c);
}

int multiply(int x, int y)
{
        int i, z = 1;

        for (i = 1; i <= y; i++)
              z = z * x;
        return z;
}
```

6.   Write a function which accepts two positive integers and returns **TRUE** if the second number lies between the square root and the cube root of the first number, inclusive; otherwise, it returns **FALSE**. For example, the numbers 64   7 will cause the function to return **TRUE** since 7 is between 8 and 4, which are the square root and cube root of 64, respectively.

7.   Write a function **factorial** which accepts a positive integer and returns the product (as a **float** number) of all positive integers up to and including that number. For example, if 3 is passed as a parameter to the function, 6 (=1 × 2 × 3) is returned; if 1 is passed as a parameter, then 1 is returned.

8.   Write a function **prodlg** that receives three **float** numbers, called **a**, **b**, and **c**, and returns the product of the two largest numbers. For example, if **a = 3**, **b = 5**, and **c = 2**, then the function will return 3 × 5 = 15.

9.   Write a function **biggest** that will receive three **int** parameters. It will determine which
      value is largest and return that value to the calling program.

10.   Criticize the following constructions:

      (a)   **int** reverse(**int** reverse);

      (b)   c funct(int a, b)

11.   What will be printed by the following program?

```
#include <stdio.h>
void main()
{
        int a, b, c;
        int func(int, int);

        a = 1;
        b = 8;
        c = func(a, b);
        printf("%d  %d  %d\n", a, b, c);
        a = func(b, a);
        printf("%d  %d  %d\n", a, b, c);
}

int func(int b, int a)
{
        int d;

        d = a * b - b * b;
        return d + b;
}
```

12.   Identify the following items in the program of Exercise 11:

      (a)   *function header*
      (b)   *function prototype*
      (c)   *function invocation*
      (d)   *function definition*

13.   What is the purpose of a *function prototype*, and how does it differ in syntax from a
      function header?

14.   Identify any errors in the following constructions. If there is no error, say no error.

(a)   **double** = trim(**double**);

(b)   int funct(int a);

     ...

     funct = a;

(c)   reverse = rvrse(word);

15.   What is printed by the following program?

```
#include <stdio.h>
void main()
{
        float a, b, c, d, e;
        float func(float, float);

        a = -2;
        b = 4;
        c = 10;
        e = 3;
        d = func(a, b);
        printf("%6.0f%6.0f%6.0f%6.0f%6.0f\n", a, b, c, d, e);
}

float func(float a, float b)
{
        float c, d, e;

        c = 4;
        d = 4;
        e = 4;
        printf("%6.0f%6.0f\n", a, b);
        c = c + a;
        e = e + b;
        printf("%6.0f%6.0f%6.0f%6.0f%6.0f\n",
                a, b, c, d, e);
        return a * b;
}
```

16.   Show exactly what is printed after each call to the function **joke**.

```
#include <stdio.h>
void main()
```

```
{
        int a, b, c, d;
        int joke(int, int, int);

        a = 5;
        b = 4;
        c = 2;
        d = joke(a, b, c);
        printf("%d   %d   %d   answer: %d\n", a, b, c, d);
        a = joke(b + 1, c, d) * 2;
        printf("%d   %d   %d   answer: %d\n", b + 1, c, d, a);
}

int joke(int x, int y, int z)
{
        int w;

        w = x + y;
        if (y > z)
                w++;
        else
                w--;
        x++;
        return w;
}
```

17.   What is printed by the following program?

```
#include <stdio.h>
void main()
{
        int a, b, c, d;
        int func(int, int);

        a = 1;
        b = 3;
        c = 5;
        d = func(a, b);
        printf("%6d%6d%6d%6d", a, b, c, d);
}

int func(int a, int b)
{
        int x, y, c;
```

```
        c = 4;
        printf("%6d%6d", c, b);
        y = b + 2;
        x = a + b;
        c = c + 11;
        return x * y;
}
```

18. Write a function **addem** which accepts as a parameter a positive integer and calculates the sum of all positive integers up to and including that number. For example, if 4 is sent to the function, then 1 + 2 + 3 + 4 = 10 is calculated and returned.

19. Repeat Exercise 18, but have the function accept a positive or negative integer. Calculate the sum of all positive integers from 1 to the number if it is positive, or the sum of all negative numbers from -1 to that number if it is negative. For example, if -5 is passed, -15 which is (-1) + (-2) + (-3) + (-4) + (-5) is returned.

20. Show exactly what is printed after each call to the function **nonsense**.

```
#include <stdio.h>
void main()
{
        int a, b, c, d;
        int nonsense(int, int, int);

        a = 5;
        b = 1;
        c = 3;
        d = nonsense(a, b, c);
        printf("%d   %d   %d   answer: %d\n", a, b, c, d);
        a = nonsense(b + 1, c, d) * 2;
        printf("%d   %d   %d   answer: %d\n", b + 1, c, d, a);
}

int nonsense(int x, int y, int z)
{
        int w;

        w = x + y + 2;
        if (y > z)
                w = w + 11;
        else
                w = w - 10;
        x = x + 1;
        return w;
```

```
}
```

21.   Each of the following program segments has an error. In each case, identify the error and show how to correct it.

```
int x[10], y;
int func(int []);
   ...
```

(a)   y = func(x[10]);

(b)   x = func(x);

22.   Write a function which receives an **int** parameter representing a person's age. The function is to return a word indicating the person's decade of life. For example, for age 18 it will return "teens"; for 25 it will return "twenties"; for 57 it will return "fifties", and so on to age 99. (Note: We have no commonly accepted word for people aged 0-9. Make one up.)

23.   Write a function which receives a parameter representing the weight of an object in pounds, in decimal form (for example, 3.50, or 0.85). The function prints the equivalent value in pounds and ounces (truncated), expressed as a string. (There are 16 ounces in a pound. 3.50 pounds would be returned as "3 pounds 8 ounces", and 0.85 pound would be returned as "0 pounds 13 ounces".)

24.   Show the output of the following program, using the datafile:

```
2      1     -2
2     -1     -9
4    -10    -11
```

```
#include <stdio.h>
void main()
{
        int i, r, s, t;
        char * decide(int, int, int);
        FILE * datafile;

        datafile = fopen("a:infile.dat", "r");
        for (i = 1; i <= 3; i++) {
                fscanf(datafile, "%d%d%d", &r, &s, &t);
                printf("%s\n", decide(r, s, t));
        }
        fclose(datafile);
}
```

```
char * decide(int r, int s, int t)
{
        if (r < 3 && s >= t)
                if ( r < s || !(t == s + 2) && s < 1)
                        return "one";
                else
                        return "two";
        else
                return "three";
}
```

25.   Write a function which will return the total amount of money in a bank account when a
       specified amount has been left on deposit at a fixed rate for a given period of time. The
       function should receive four parameters, the amount deposited, the rate of simple interest
       (not compounded within a year), the year of deposit, and the year of withdrawal. (The
       date of deposit and the date of withdrawal are the same month and day.)

Section 7-2   Using Pointers as Parameters

26.   Write a C function that will receive four parameters, each of which is a pointer to a **float**
       variable. If the mean (average) of the first two numbers is greater than the mean of the
       second two numbers, the variables pointed to by the parameters will be set to 8.6.
       Otherwise, the variables will be set to 0.9.

27.   Explain the difference between sending a parameter to a function by *value* and by
       reference.

28.   Write a complete C program to analyze a set of groups of student's scores. Each group
       (you don't know how many groups there are) consists of a student name (15 characters
       maximum) and three integers (on a separate line from the name). The first two integers are
       exam scores; the last integer is the final exam score.

       You should write and use the following:

•   A function called **readdata**, to read a group of data.

•   A function called **errorfree**, which will receive a single integer grade and return it,
     corrected if necessary, as follows:

       If the grade is negative, make it the equivalent positive value (e.g., -75 becomes
       75);

       If it is greater than 100, subtract 100 from it as many times as necessary so that it is between 0 and 100. (Note: if no changes are made, the function simply returns the original value.)

- A function called **finalgrade**, which computes a student's final numeric grade from the corrected data on the following basis: each exam counts 25%, and the final counts 50%.

For each student you should print, on a single line, the name, exam scores (corrected), final exam score, and final number grade. This grade should include one decimal place. After these figures have been printed for each student, skip a few lines and print the highest final grade and the name of the student who received it. Provide headings for the output columns and labels for the data below the table.

29.   What will be the output of the following program?

```
#include <stdio.h>
void main()
{
        int a, b, c;
        void changes (int *, int *, int *);

        a = 3;
        b = -5;
        c = 2;
        printf("%d   %d  %d\n", a, b, c);
        changes(&a, &b, &c);
        printf("%d   %d  %d\n", a, b, c);
        changes(&c, &a, &b);        /* note order of arguments */
        printf("%d   %d  %d\n", a, b, c);
}

void changes(int *px, int *py, int *pz)
{
        int d;

        d = *px + *py;
        *pz = d + 1;
        *px = d - 2 * *py;
}
```

30.   Rewrite the following function so that it does not use pointers. Following the header, insert a comment that tells what the function does.

```
void raise(float x, int p, float *presult)
{
```

```
        int c = 1;

        *presult = 1;
        while (c <= p) {
                *presult = *presult * x;
                c++;
        }
}
```

31.   Show what is printed by the following program:

```
#include <stdio.h>
void main()
{
        int a, b, c;
        void sub(int *, int *);

        a = 3;
        b = 6;
        sub(&a, &c);
        printf("%d   %d %d\n", a, b, c);
        sub(&b, &c);
        printf("%d   %d %d\n", a, b, c);
}

void sub(int *px, int *py)
{
        *px = *px + 1;
        *py = *px + 3;
}
```

32.   Write a function **intquot** which accepts two integers, **x**, and **y**, and a pointer to an integer
       z, and sets **z** equal to the quotient of **x** divided by **y** if the quotient is integral, or to the
       next higher integer if the quotient is not integral. For example, if **x** is 7 and **y** is 2, then **z**
       is set equal to 4, the next integer after 3.5.

33.   What is printed by the following program?

```
#include <stdio.h>
void main()
{
        float a, b, c, perfect;
        float quiz(float, float, float);
        void fail(float *, float *);
```

```
            a = 3;
            b = 2;
            perfect = 100;
            while (perfect >= 100) {
                    c = quiz(perfect, a, b);
                    fail(&b, &c);
                    printf("%6.0f%6.0f%6.0f%8.0f\n",
                            a, b, c, perfect);
                    if (c > 30)
                            perfect = perfect / 2;
            }
            printf("%12.0f\n", perfect);
}

float quiz(float superb, float excellent, float good)
{
        float f;

        f = 50;
        if (superb >= excellent)
                f = 10 * excellent * good;
        else
                f = f / excellent;
        return f;
}

void fail(float *pgrade, float *pmark)
{
        *pgrade = *pgrade * 2;
        *pmark = *pmark / 2;
}
```

34.   Here is a program and some data. Show what is printed. The data file contains:

```
6   7   5   14   15   16   9   3   2
```

```
#include <stdio.h>
void main()
{
        int x, y, z;
        void swap(int *, int *, int *);
        FILE * infile;

        infile = fopen("data", "r");
        x = 5;
```

```
                y = 3;
                z = 4;
                while (fscanf(infile, "%d%d%d", &x, &y, &z) == 3) {
                        printf("%d   %d   %d\n", x, y, z);
                        swap(&x, &y, &z);
                        printf("%d   %d   %d\n", x, y, z);
                }
                printf("%d   %d   %d\n", x, y, z);
                fclose(infile);
        }


        void swap(int *pa, int *pb, int *pc)
        {
                if (*pa > *pc) {
                        *pa = *pb;
                        *pb = *pc;
                        *pc = *pa;
                }
        }
```

35.   Show exactly what is printed by the following program:

```
        #include <stdio.h>
        void main()
        {
                int a, b, c, d;
                void sub(int *, int *);

                a = 5;
                b = 10;
                c = 15;
                d = 20;
                sub(&a, &c);
                printf("%d   %d   %d   %d\n", a, b, c, d);
                sub(&b, &d);
                printf("%d   %d   %d   %d\n", a, b, c, d);
        }

        void sub(int *pd, int *pc)
        {
                int a, b;

                a = 1;
                b = 2;
                *pc = 3;
```

```
                        *pd = 4;
            }
```

36.   Define the following terms: *input parameter, output parameter, input/output parameter, local variable*. Give an example of each of these, if possible, from Examples 29 and 33.

37.   Write a function which accepts two positive integers and returns the largest integer exponent of the second number which will produce a result less than or equal to the first number. For example, 100   2 will return 6, because 2 to the 6th power is less than 100, but 2 to the 7th power is not.

38   Write a function which accepts three parameters—two numbers, **a** and **b** and a pointer to a string, **c**. The function calculates and prints the quotient of **a** divided by **b,** if **b** is not zero. The string **c** is for a comment to state if the denominator is zero. For example if **a** is 6 and **b** is 2 the function prints 3 (6 / 2 = 3), while if **b** is 0 the function assigns "Error: Division by zero" to the string **c**.

39.   What is printed by the following program? Use the following sets of data values:

```
    1  2  3     4  3  2     4  4  4     4  5  4     0  7  5     0  0  0
```

```c
#include <stdio.h>
void main()
{
        int num1, num2, num3, big;
        int max(int, int, int);

        scanf("%d%d%d", &num1, &num2, &num3);
        while (num1 != 0 || num2 != 0 || num3 != 0) {
                big = max(num1, num2, num3);
                printf("%d\n", big);
                scanf("%d%d%d", &num1, &num2, &num3);
        }
}

/* function returns max of three values */
int max(int val1, int val2, int val3)
{
        int big;

        if (val1 >= val2)
                big = val1;
        else
                big = val2;
```

```
        if (big < val3)
                big = val3;
        return big;
}
```

40   What is printed by the following program? Use the following sets of data values:

        2 3 4   5 5 6   7 5 9   10 -10 22   0 0 0

```
#include <stdio.h>
void main()
{
        int num1, num2, num3;
        void sort(int *, int *, int *);

        scanf("%d%d%d", &num1, &num2, &num3);
        while (num1 != 0 || num2 != 0 || num3 != 0) {
                sort(&num1, &num2, &num3);
                printf("%d   %d   %d\n", num1, num2, num3);
                scanf("%d%d%d", &num1, &num2, &num3);
        }
}


void sort(int *val1, int *val2, int *val3)
{
        int temp;

        if (*val1 >= *val2) {
                temp = *val1;
                *val1 = *val2;
                *val2 = temp;
        }
        if (*val2 > *val3) {
                temp = *val2;
                *val2 = * val3;
                *val3 = temp;
        }
        if (*val1 > *val2) {
                temp = *val1;
                *val1 = *val2;
                *val2 = temp;
        }
}
```

41.   What is printed by the following program?

```
#include <stdio.h>
void main()
{
        int num, boolean;
        void func(float);

        num = 0;
        boolean = num == 0;
        boolean ? printf("TRUE\n") : printf("FALSE\n");
        func(num);
        printf("%d\n", num);
}

void func(float x)
{
        x++;
        printf("%f\n", x);
}
```

42.   Correct the errors in the following program

```
#include <stdio.h>
#define N 10
#define DOUBLE 2 * N
void main()
{
        int x, y, z;
        int fun(int, int, float);

        x = N;
        y = DOUBLE;
        z = 66;
        x = fun(x, y, z);
        printf("%d   %d   %d\n", x, y, z);
}

int fun(int a, int b, float *c)
{
        a = a + 1;
        b = b + 2;
        *c = *c + 3;
        return a + b + *c;
}
```

Section 7-3   Arrays in Functions

43.   What is the effect of the following function?

```
#define TRUE 1
#define FALSE 0

int equal(int arr[])
{
        int i;

        for (i = 0; i < 10; i++)
                if (arr[i] == i)
                        return TRUE;
        return FALSE;
}
```

44.   (a) Write a function **sumpart** that has three parameters:

(1) an array of 10 **float** numbers called **arr**
(2) an **int** parameter **lim1**
(3) an **int** parameter **lim2**

sumpart returns a **float** number containing the sum of all the elements in **arr** from subscript **lim1** to subscript **lim2**, inclusive.

Example: if **arr** is   1 2 3 9 5 18 9 10
and **lim1** is 4
and **lim2** is 7

then **sumpart** returns 55 which is equal to 9 + 5 + 18 + 23

(b) Write a function **partsum** that has three parameters:

(1) a two-dimensional array called **arr**, of **float** numbers. **arr** has 5 rows and 10 columns.
(2) an **int** parameter **rowx**
(3) an **int** parameter **coly**

partsum returns a **float** number containing the sum of all the elements in **rowx** of **arr** and **coly** of **arr**.

Example: if **arr** is

1	2	3	9	5	12	23	89	10	23
3	-1	9	21	22	23	24	25	29	99
-2	90	77	72	67	43	33	98	-10	0
83	701	79	-1	32	43	54	65	79	80
103	81	-9	-1	-2	-3	-4	-5	-9	0

and **rowx** is 2
and **rowy** is 7

then **partsum** returns 384 which is equal to the sum of the elements in row 2 and those in column 7:

$$3 + (-1) + 9 + 21 + 22 + 23 + 24 + 25 + 29 + 99$$
$$+ 23 + 24 + 33 + 54 + (-4) = 384$$

45.   What is printed by the following program? Use the following data:

5   3   4   8   9   2

```
#include <stdio.h>
void main()
{
        int arr[6], i, number;
        int sumsome(int [], int, int);

        for (i = 0; i < 6; i++)
                scanf("%d", &arr[i]);
        number = sumsome(arr, 2, 3);
        printf("%d\n", number);
}

int sumsome(int arr[], int i, int j)
{
        int k, num;

        num = 0;
        for (k = i; k <= j; k++)
                num = num + arr[k];
        return num;
}
```

46.   Write a function called **func**, which takes as parameters an array of integers, called **arr** and the number of elements in the array, called **n**. The function returns the smallest positive (but nonzero) value in the array. If there are no positive values, it returns zero.

47.   Write a function called **hiloavg** that accepts two parameters: an integer **n** and an **int**

array **arr**.

hiloavg does the following:
(a) It finds the largest and smallest elements within the first **n** elements of **arr**, and prints these values (within the function).
(b) It returns the average (as a real number) of the largest and smallest elements.

For example: If **arr** contains 8 6 5 4 10 -1 3 and **n = 7;**, then if we write **ans = hiloavg(arr, n);** the function will print high = 10 and low = -1 and will return 4.5 (the average of 10 and -1) to the calling program.

48.   Write a function **settoten** that accepts three parameters:

1)   an **int** array **arr**
2)   the value of **n**
3)   a counter **k**

and does the following:

(a)   All elements of the **arr** array that were greater than 10 are set equal to 10.
(b)   All elements of the **arr** array that were originally 10 or less remain unchanged.
(c)   **k** is set to the number of elements that were changed.

For example: if **arr** contains 15 10 7 11 4 -1 235 and **n = 7;**, then after we execute the statement **settoten(arr, n, k);** the array **arr** will contain 10 10 7 10 4 -1 10 and 3.

49.   Write a function **fixit** that receives two parameters:

1)   an array **arr** of 50 integers
2)   a number **n** between 1 and 48

fixit doubles the elements of **arr** between 0 and **n** and triples the elements of **arr** between **n + 1** and 49.

50.   Write a function called **putpart** which receives two parameters:

1)   a 10-element array **arr** of **int**
2)   an integer **n**

putpart adds 5 to every element in **arr** whose subscript is less than **n** and adds 10 to all other elements of the array.

For example: if **arr** is 3 4 5 6 7 8 9 10 1 2 and **n** is 4, then **putpart** changes **arr** to 8 9 10 16 17 18 19 20 11 12

51.   Write a function **assign**, which receives three parameters:

   1)   a 5 by 6 two-dimensional array **arr** of **int**
   2)   an integer **n**
   3)   a 6-element array **arr2** of **int**

   The function places the **n**th row of **arr** into **arr2**.

   For example: if **arr** is

1	2	3	4	5	6
-1	-2	-3	-4	-5	-6
21	22	23	24	25	26
90	91	92	93	94	95
7	9	1	3	4	5

   and **n** is 3,
   then **assign** gives **arr2** the values 21   22   23   24   25   26

52.   A main function will read a number **n** and then a set of **n** names into an array called
        person. The main function uses a function **alpha** to process the names as shown below.
        At the call to the function, the array **person** and **n** (the number of elements to be
        searched) have values; **alpha** sets **first** to the first name on the list and **last** to the last
        name on the list. (You may assume that $n \geq 2$ and that no two names on the list are the
        same.) Write the function **alpha**.

```
#include <stdio.h>
#include <string.h>
void main()
{
        char person[100][30], first[30], last[30];
        int i, n;
        /* function prototype for alpha goes here */

        scanf("%d", &n);
        for (i = 0; i < n; i++)
                scanf("%s", person[i]);
        alpha(person, n, first, last);
        printf("First name = %s\n", first);
        printf("Last name = %s\n", last);
}

/* function alpha goes here */
```

53.   The following program has an infinite loop. What causes the infinite loop? Tell how the
        difficulty can be corrected.

```c
#include <stdio.h>
int a, b, c, d, i, arr[50];
void sub(int *, int *, int *);

void main()
{
        a = 3;
        b = 10;
        c = 0;
        i = 0;
        while (i < 50) {
                scanf("%d", &arr[i]);
                printf("%d\n", arr[i]);
                sub(&arr[i], &b, &c);
                d = b * arr[i];
                i++;
        }
}

void sub(int *px, int * py, int *pz)
{
        i = 1;
        while ( i <= 2) {
                *py = *px * i;
                *pz = *pz + *py;
                i++;
        }
}
```

54.   Below are two techniques to print a set of 100 book titles from a function. Explain the difference in the two methods. Which technique is superior? Why? Will the other work?

(a)
```c
#include <stdio.h>
#define N 100
void main()
{
        int i;
        char title[N][80];
        void printall(char [][80]);

        for (i = 0; i < N; i++)
                scanf("%s", title[i]);
        printall(title);
}
```

```
        void printall(char name[][80])
        {
                int i;

                for (i = 0; i < N; i++)
                        printf("%s\n", name[i]);
        }
```

(b)   ```
        #include <stdio.h>
        #define N 100
        void main()
        {
                int i;
                char title[N][80];
                void printtitle(char []);

                for (i = 0; i < N; i++) {
                        scanf("%s", title[i]);
                        printtitle(title[i]);
                }
        }

        void printtitle(char name[])
        {
                printf("%s\n", name);
        }
```
```

CHAPTER 8 - POINTERS AND INDIRECTION

Section 8-1 Pointers and Indirection

1.   Describe the purpose of the *address* operator (**&**) and the *indirection* operator (*****). How can they be distinguished from the similar looking *bit-wise and* and *multiplication* operators?

2.   What is the result of the following program segment?

```
int x, y, *p, *q;

p = &x;
q = &y;
x = 5;
*q = *p;
printf("%d   %d\n", x, y);
```

3.   Show what is printed by the following program segment.

```
int x = 5, y = 6, *p, *q, temp;

p = &x;
q = &y;
printf("%d    %d\n", x, y);
temp = *p;
*p = *q;
*q = temp;
printf("%d    %d\n", *p, *q);
```

4.   Explain the result of the following program segment:

```
int x = 8, y = 8, *p = &x, *q = &y;

printf("%d  %d  %d  %d  %d\n",
         x - y, *p - *q, x - *q, p - q, (int) p - (int) q);
```

5.   What is the value of **sum** after each of the following program segments? Assume the following declarations:

```
int    a[10] = {1, 2, 3, 4, 5, 0, 0, 1,1, 1},
       i, sum = 0, *p = a;
```

    (a)   **for** (i = 0; i < 10; i++)
                sum = sum + a[i];

    (b)   **for** (; p < &a[10]; p++)
                sum = sum + *p;

    (c)   **for** (i = 0; i < 10; i++)
                sum = sum + *(a + i);

6.   What is the result of the following program?

```
#include <stdio.h>
void main()
{
        int i, a[10], *p, *q;

        for (i = 0; i < 10; i++) {
                *(a + i) = 10 - i * 2;
                printf("%d ", a[i]);
        }
        printf("\n");
        p = a;
        *(p + 5) = 99;
        q = p + 5;
        p++;
        *p = 99;
        *q = 99;
        for (i = 0; i < 10; i++)
                printf("%d ", a[i]);
}
```

7.*   After executing the following program, what is the numeric value of each of the expressions shown below?

```
void main()
{
        int i, j, k, a[3], *p, **q, *r, *s;

        i = 3;
        p = &i;
        q = &p;
        for (k = 0; k < 3; k++)
                a[k] = k;
        s = &a[1];
```

```
        }
```

(a)	*p	(b)	**q
(c)	p == &i	(d)	** &p
(e)	*(r = &i)	(f)	q == p
(g)	*q == p	(h)	*(a + 2)
(i)	*s	(j)	*(s + 1)

8.*   What will be printed by the following program?

```
#include <stdio.h>
void main()
{
        int i, k[4], *p, **pp;

        pp = &p;
        i = 0;
        p = k;
        while (i < 4)
                *p++ = i++;
        p -= 4;
        **pp += 100;
        *pp += 1;
        **pp += 200;
        printf("%d  %d  %d  %d  %d  %d  %d\n",
                        k[0], k[1], k[2], k[3], *p, **pp, i);
}
```

9.*   What will be printed by the following program?

```
#include <stdio.h>
void main()
{
        int i, j, k, a[3], *p[3], **q, **r, *s, *t;

        i = 33;
        j = 55;
        k = 77;

        for (j = 0; j < 3; j++) {
                a[j] = j;
                p[j] = &a[j];
        }

        s = &a[1];
```

```
        q = &p[1];
        t = *q + 1;
        r = q + 1;

        for (j = 0; j < 4; j++)
                printf("%d   ", a[j]);
        printf("\n");
        for (j = 0; j < 3; j++)
                printf("%d   ", *p[j]);
        printf("\n");
        printf("%d   %d   %d    %d\n", **q, **r, *s, *t);
    }
```

10*   After executing the program in Exercise 9, what is the numeric value of each of the expressions shown below?

(a)   **p   (b)   *p[1]
(c)   *&a[2]   (d)   *(*r = &k)
(e)   *(a + 2)   (f)   *s
(g)   *(s + 1)   (h)   **p + 1

CHAPTER 9 - ARRAYS

Section 9-1   One-Dimensional Arrays

1.   State the value of the subscript used for the array **a** in each of the last five statements of the program segment below.

```
int a[10], i;
    ...
i = 5;
a[6] = 12;
a[i] = 9;
a[i - 2] = i;
a[i / 2] = 1 + 1;
a[a[i]] = 17;
```

2.   Determine the number of the elements in each of the following arrays. What is the lower bound and what is the upper bound of the included subscripts?

```
#define N 15;
int     a[10], b[N];
```

3.   Describe the output from the following program segment:

```
int a, b, c, d, e, i, arr[6];
    ...
a = 1;
b = 2;
c = 3;
d = 4;
e = 5;
for (i = 0; i < 6; i++)
        arr[i] = 10 * i;
printf("%d  %d  %d  %d  %d\n", arr[a], arr[b], arr[c], arr[d], arr[e]);
```

4.   What will be printed in each of the following cases?

(a)
```
int a[10], i;
    ...
for (i = 0; i < 10; i++)
        a[i] = 0;
```

   (i)   `printf("%d\n", a[0]);`

      (ii)   printf("%d\n", a[9]);

(b)   **int** b[10], i, y = 2;

```
          ...
     for (i = 0; i < 10; i++)
             b[i] = 0;
     b[6] = 1;
     b[7] = 1;
     b[8] = 1;
     b[9] = 1;
```

      (i)   printf("%d\n", b[1] * b[9]);

      (ii)   printf("%d\n", b[2] + b[6] + b[9]);

      (iii)   printf("%d\n", b[y] + 1);

      (iv)   printf("%d\n", b[y+1]);

5.   State what will be printed by each of the following program segments. Use the following data:

           10   20   30   40   50

(a)   **int** a[5], i;

```
          ...
     for (i = 0; i < 5; i++) {
             scanf("%d", &a[i]);
             printf("%d\n", a[i]);
     }
```

(b)   **int** a[5], b, i;

```
          ...
     for (i = 0; i < 5; i++)
             a[i] = 2 * i;
     b = 1;
     for (i = 0; i < 5; i++)
             printf("%d   %d\n", i, a[i]);
     for (i = 0; i < 5; i++)
             printf("%d   %d\n", i, a[b]);
```

(c)   **int** a[5], b[5], i;

```
          ...
     for (i = 0; i < 5; i++)
```

```
                a[i] = 0;
        for (i = 0; i < 5; i++)
                b[i] = i;
        for (i = 0; i < 5; i++)
                a[i] = b[i];
        for (i = 0; i < 5; i++)
                printf("%d   %d   %d\n", i, a[i], b[i]);
```

6.   What will be printed by each of the following program segments? If a memory location
     has not been given a value, indicate its value with a question mark (?). Use the following
     data for each part:

                    1   2   3   4   5   6   7   8

(a)   **int** a[10], i, j;
           ...
```
        for (i = 0; i < 10; i++)
                a[1] = 0;
        for (j = 0; j < 8; j++)
                scanf("%d", &a[j]);
        for (i = 0; i < 10; i++)
                printf("%d\n", a[i]);
```

(b)   **int** a[10], i, j;
           ...
```
        for (j = 0; j < 8; j++)
                scanf("%d", &a[j]);
        j = 7;
        for (i = 0; i < 10; i++)
                printf("%d\n", a[j]);
```

(c)   **int** a[10], i, j;
           ...
```
        for (i = 0; i < 10; i++)
                a[1] = 0;
        for (j = 0; j < 9; j++)
                a[j] = 1;
        for (i = 0; i < 10; i++)
                printf("%d   %d\n", i, a[i]);
```

(d)   **int** a[10], i, j;
           ...
```
        for (i = 0; i < 9; i++)
                a[i] = 0;
        for (j = 0; j < 10; j++)
```

```
            a[i] = 1;
    for (i = 0; i < 10; i++)
          printf("%d   %d\n", i, a[i]);
```

7.   Suggest meaningful identifiers for each of the following arrays and for the subscript in each of them.

(a) An array for the final exam grades of all students in the class.
(b) An array to determine the number of students in each of the following grade ranges on the final exam:

grade range	0-10	11-20	21-30	31-40	...	91-100
array subscript	1	2	3	4		10

8.   What happens when you refer to an array element which is outside of the declared array?

9.   What is the difference, if any, between the two parts below? Show the values stored in the two arrays after each part is executed. Use the following data:

```
   1   2   3   4   5   6   7   8

   int a[4], b[4], i;
```

(a)   ```
      for (i = 0; i < 4; i++)
            scanf("%d", &a[i]);
      for (i = 0; i < 4; i++)
            scanf("%d", &b[i]);
      ```
(b)   ```
      for (i = 0; i < 4; i++)
            scanf("%d%d", &a[i], &b[i]);
      ```

10.   What will be printed by the following program segments? What difference is there in the outputs of Part (a) and (b)? Use the following declarations and initializations for each part:

```
      int a[10], x, i;
      ...
      for (i = 0; i < 5; i++)
            a[i] = 5;
```

(a)   ```
      for (i = 0; i < 5; i++) {
            a[i] = a[i] + a[2];
            printf("%d   ", a[i]);
      }
      ```

(b)   ```
      x = a[2];
      for (i = 0; i < 5; i++) {
      ```

```
                    a[i] = a[i] + x;
                    printf("%d   ", a[i]);
            }
```

11.   Write a program segment to increase the value of each element of the 10-element array
        arr by the value currently in **arr[3]**.

12.   Write a program segment to set the last 10 elements of array **b** equal to the first 10
        elements of array **a**, respectively. Assume that **a** and **b** are declared as follows:

            int a[20], b[20];

13.   Write a program segment which will place twice the value of the last 10 elements of array
        a into the first 10 elements of array **b**. For example, if **a** and **b** are declared as:

            int a[100], b[10];

        and **a[99]** and **a[98]** have values -4 and +12, your segment will place -8 and +24 into
        b[0] and **b[1]**, respectively.

14.   What is wrong with the following program segment? Show how the difficulty can be
        corrected. Will an error message be produced?

```
            int a[10], i, j;
                ...
            for (i = 1; i < 10; i++) {
                    a[i] = i;
                    printf("%d  ", a[i]);
                    a[i] = a[i] + 1;
                    a[i + 1] = a[i];
            }
            for (i = 0; i < 10; i++)
                    printf("%d\n", a[i]);
```

15.   What is printed by the following program?

```
            #include <stdio.h>
            void main()
            {
                    int a[7], i, temp, n, newnum;

                    a[0] = 1;
                    a[1] = 5;
                    a[2] = 3;
                    a[3] = 2;
```

```
                        a[4] = 6;
                        a[5] = 7;
                        a[6] = 98;
                        n = 7;
                        newnum = n / 2;
                        for (i = 0; i < newnum; i++) {
                                temp = a[i];
                                a[i] = a[n - i + 1];
                                a[n - i + 1] = temp;
                                printf("%d   %d   %d\n", a[i], i, temp);
                        }
                        for (i = 0; i < n; i++)
                                printf("%d   ", a[i]);
                }
```

16.   Write a complete program to read an unknown number (at least one but no more than 50) of integers. Print the integers in the order in which they were read in. Find the average of the integers. Print the average and the largest integer which is less than the average. Could this problem be solved without using an array? Explain.

17.   What output will the following program produce? The data file contains 3 9 2 4 7.

```
            #include <stdio.h>
            void main()
            {
                    int numbers[5], i;
                    FILE * dfile;

                    dfile = fopen("data.dat", "r");
                    for (i = 0; i < 5; i++)
                            numbers[i] = 0;
                    for (i = 2; i <= 4; i++)
                            fscanf(dfile, "%d", &numbers[i]);
                    for (i = 0; i < 5; i++)
                            printf("%d\n", numbers[i]);
                    fclose(dfile);
            }
```

18.   What output will the following program produce? The data file contains

            3 9 2 4 7 0 18 12 9 1

```
            #include <stdio.h>
            void main()
            {
```

```
            int numbers[10], i;
            FILE * dfile;

            dfile = fopen("data.dat", "r");
            for (i = 0; i < 10; i++)
                    numbers[i] = 0;
                    i = 0;
                    while (fscanf(dfile, "%d", &numbers[i]) != EOF) {
                            printf("%d    ", numbers[i]);
                            i++;
                    }
                    i = 0;
                    do {
                            printf("%d    ", numbers[i]);
                            i++;
                    } while (numbers[i] != 0);
                    fclose(dfile);
            }
```

19.   An error will occur during the execution of the program below which may or may not
       show up in the output. Indicate the nature of the error and how to avoid it. Assume the
       data file contains the following:

           7   2   2   4   1   7   1   16   8   3   2   10

```
       #include <stdio.h>
       void main()
       {
               int x[10], n[10], i;
               FILE * dfile;

               dfile = fopen("data.dat", "r");
               for (i = 0; i < 10; i++)
                       x[i] = 0;
               for (i = 0; i < 10; i++) {
                       fscanf(dfile, "%d", &n[i]);
                       x[n[i]]++;
                       printf("%d   %d   ", n[i], x[i]);
               }
               printf("\n");
               for (i = 0; i < 10; i++)
                       printf("%d   ", x[i]);
               fclose(dfile);
       }
```

20.   Below is part of a program which is to read a maximum of 50 integers using the header method. The program is to determine the largest and smallest values. Fill in the missing portion so that the program does this task. (Is an array necessary to do this task?)

```
#include <stdio.h>
void main()
{
        int number[50], n, large, small, i;

        scanf('%d", &n);
        for (i = 0; i < n; i++)
                scanf("%d", &number[i]);

        /* Missing portion goes here. */

        printf("The largest value is %d\n", large);
        printf("The smallest value is %d\n", small);
}
```

21.   Assume **n** integers have been read into an array **a**, which is declared as follows:

```
int a[50];
```

Also assume **n** is guaranteed to be less than 50. Write the instructions needed to move each of the first **n** elements in array **a** to the next element position in the array and then fill the first element with 0. Use a **for** loop and do not use any variables other than the array **a**, the index **i** and the header **n**.

Example: n = 5;

before		after	
a[0]	9	a[0]	0
a[1]	3	a[1]	9
a[2]	1	a[2]	3
a[3]	2	a[3]	1
a[4]	6	a[4]	2
a[5]	...	a[5]	6
...		...	
a[49]		a[49]	

22.   Write a C program that will read an unknown number of data lines from a data set; each line contains a person's name (a string of no more than 10 characters) and weight. Compute the average weight of all persons listed in the data set. Print the names of all persons who are within 20 pounds of the average weight (i.e., 20 pounds more or less). For example, if the average weight is 150 pounds, then print all the names of all persons

who weigh between 130 and 170 pounds, inclusive. Use arrays to do this program and do not read the input data set more than once.

23.   Show exactly what will be printed by the program shown below. Assume that *mydata.dat* contains the following entries: 5   6   1   2.

```c
#include <stdio.h>
void main()
{
        int a[6], i, x;
        FILE * datafile;

        datafile = fopen("mydata.dat", "r");
        for (i = 0; i < 6; i++)
                a[i] = 7;
        x = 0;
        i = 1;
        while (!feof(datafile)) {
                a[i] = a[i] + x;
                fscanf(datafile, "%d", &x);
        }
        for (i = 0; i < 6; i++)
                printf("%d\n", a[i]);
        fclose(datafile);

}
```

24.   Show exactly what is printed by the following program.

```c
#include <stdio.h>
void main()
{
        int x[5], i, sub;

        x[2] = 3;
        x[1] = 7;
        x[4] = 9;
        x[0] = -5;
        x[3] = 5;
        for (i = 0; i < 5; i++)
                printf("%d   ", x[i]);
        printf("\n");
        for (sub = 1; sub < 5; sub++)
                x[sub - 1] = sub * x[sub];
        x[4] = 17;
        for (sub = 0; sub < 5; sub++)
```

```
            printf("%d    %d\n", sub, x[sub]);
}
```

25.   Show exactly what is printed by the following program.

```
#include <stdio.h>
void main()
{
        char x[5], y;
        int i;

        x[4] = 'c';
        x[1] = 'w';
        y = 'y';
        for (i = 0; i < 4; i++)
                x[i] = y;
        printf("%c%c%c%c\n", x[1], x[2], x[3], x[4]);
        x[3]++;
        x[4]--;
        for (i = 0; i < 5; i++)
                printf("%c\n", x[i]);
}
```

26.   Show what is printed by the following program. The data values to be used are as follows:

```
3    6    9    12    0    15    2    5    8    11
```

```
#include <stdio.h>
void main()
{

        char *x;
        int month;
        char *season(int);

        do {
                printf("Enter any number ");
                scanf("%d", &month);
                x = season(month);
                printf("%d    %s\n", month, x);
        } while (month != 8);
}

char *season(int month)
{
```

```
        char *choices[5] = {"winter", "spring", "summer", "fall", "error"};

        if (month == 1 || month == 2 || month == 12)
                return choices[0];
        else if (month >= 3 && month <= 5)
                return choices[1];
        else if (month >= 6 && month <= 8)
                return choices[2];
        else if (month >= 9 && month <= 11)
                return choices[3];
        else
                return choices[4];
}
```

27.   Trace the following program and show exactly what is printed. The file on the disk *extname.dat* consists of a single line containing:

        1   5   3   2   6   7   98

```
        #include <stdio.h>
        #define Z 7
        void main()
        {
                int number[Z], j, k, n, t;
                FILE * numberfile;

                numberfile = fopen("extname.dat", "r");
                for (j = 0; j < Z; j++)
                        fscanf(numberfile, "%d", &number[j]);
                n = Z;
                k = n / 2;
                for (j = 0; j < k; j++) {
                        t = number[j];
                        number[j] = number[n - j - 1];
                        number[n - j - 1] = t;
                }
                for (j = 0; j < Z; j++)
                        printf("%d  ", number[j]);
        }
```

28.   State what will be printed by the following program:

```
        #include <stdio.h>
        #include <math.h>
        void main()
```

```
{
        int arr[10], x, y, i;

        for (i = 0; i < 10; i++)
                arr[i] = 0;
        x = 4;
        y = 7;
        arr[x] = x + y;
        arr[x + 1] = arr[x] + 1;
        arr[y - x] = (x - y) * (x - y);
        arr[x * x - y] = 2 * 2 * 2;
        arr[floor(sqrt(x))] = ceil(sqrt(y));
        for (i = 0; i < 10; i++)
                printf("%d  ", arr[i]);
}
```

Section 9-2 Two-Dimensional Arrays

29.   Suggest a meaningful identifier for a two-dimensional array for the sales of the various departments of the several branches of a chain store. Also suggest identifiers for its two subscripts.

30.   How many elements are there in each of the following arrays?

        int   a[2][10], b[1][5], c[2][3][4];

31.   To the right is a diagram of array **x**.

        int   x[3][4], i, j;

Parts (a) - (c) of this question present three ways of printing the values in the array. In each case show exactly what is printed.

x	0	1	2	3
0	3	6	9	12
1	15	18	21	24
2	27	30	33	36

(a)
```
for (i = 0; i < 3; i++)
        for (j = 0; i < 4; i++)
                printf("%d ", x[i][j]);
```

(b)
```
for (j = 3; j >=0; j--)
        for (i = 0; i < 3; i++)
                printf("%d ", x[i][j]);
```

(c)   **for** (j = 0; j < 4; j++)
                   for (i = 0; i < 3; i++)
                          printf("%d ", x[i][j]);

32.   What is printed by the following program? Use the following data:

        0   5   6   4   8   47   16   13   7098   629

```
#include <stdio.h>
void main()
{
        int x[3][2], i, j;

        for (i = 0; i < 3; i++)
                for (j = 0; j < 2; j++)
                        scanf("%d", &x[i][j]);
        printf("%d\n", x[2][0]);
}
```

33.   What is printed by the following program?

```
#include <stdio.h>
void main()
{
        int a[5][2], i, j, k;

        for (i = 0; i < 5; i++)
                for (j = 0; j <2; j++)
                        a[i][j] = -1;
        for (j = 0; j < 2; j++) {
                k = 2;
                i = 1;
                while (i < 5 && j != i) {
                        k--;
                        if (i > k)
                                a[i][j] = i * j;
                        else
                                a[i][j] = i + j;
                        i++;
                }
                printf("%d   %d   %d\n", i, j, k);
        }
        for (i = 0; i < 5; i++)
```

```
                    for (j = 0; j < 2; j++)
                            printf("%d   ", a[i][j]);
            printf("\nsecond\n");
            for (j = 0; j < 2; j++)
                    for (i = 0; i < 5; i++)
                            printf("%d   ", a[i][j]);
    }
```

34.   What is printed by the following program?

```
        #include <stdio.h>
        void main()
        {
                int x[3][2], j;

                x[0][1] = 8;
                x[1][1] = 9;
                x[2][1] = 1;
                x[0][0] = 3;
                x[1][0] = 6;
                x[2][0] = 4;
                for (j = 0; j < 3; j++)
                        printf("%d\n", x[j][1]);
        }
```

35.   What values are stored in array **x** after the following statements are executed?

```
        #include <stdio.h>
        void main()
        {
                int x[4][2], i, j;

                for (i = 0; i < 4; i++)
                        for (j = 0; j < 2; j++)
                                x[i][j] = 6;
                i = 1;
                while (i < 4) {
                        for (j = 1; j >= 0; j--)
                                x[i][j] = x[i][j] + 2;
                        i = i + 3;
                }
        }
```

36.   For each part of this question, show exactly what is printed:

(a)   #include <stdio.h>
        void main()
        {
                int a[4][4], i, j;

                for (i = 0; i < 4; i++)
                        for (j = 0; j < 4; j++)
                                a[i][j] = 13;
                for (j = 0; j < 4; j++)
                        for (i = 0; i < 4; i++)
                                if (i - j == 0)
                                        a[i][j] = a[i][j] + i;
                                else if (i - j > 0)
                                        a[i][j] = j;
                for (j = 0; j < 4; j++)
                        for (i = 3; i >= 0; i--)
                                printf("%d   ", a[i][j]);
        }

(b)   #include <stdio.h>
        void main()
        {
                int b[4][4], i, j;

                for (i = 0; i < 4; i++)
                        for (j = 0; j < 4; j++)
                                b[i][j] = 9;
                for (j = 3; j >= 0; j--)
                        for (i = 3; i >=0; i--)
                                if (i - j < 0)
                                        b[i][j] = b[i][j] + j;
                                else if (i - j == 0)
                                        b[i][j] = j;
                for (i = 0; i < 4; i++) {
                        for (j = 0; j < 4; j++)
                                printf("%4d", b[i][j]);
                        printf("\n");
                }
        }

37.   For each part of this question show exactly what is printed. Also draw a picture of the
       array at the end of each part. Use the following data:

             1   2   3   4   5   6   7   8   9   10

(a)   ```
        #include <stdio.h>
        void main()
        {
                int a[2][4], i, j, k, m;

                for (m = -1; m <= 2; m++)
                        for (k = 1; k <= 2; k++) {
                                i = 2 - k;
                                j = m + 1;
                                scanf("%d", &a[i][j]);
                                printf("%d\n", a[i][j]);
                        }
        }
        ```

(b)     ```
        #include <stdio.h>
        void main()
        {
                int b[4][2], i, j, k, m;

                for (i = -2; i <= 1; i++)
                        for (j = 3; j <= 4; j++) {
                                k  = i + 2;
                                m = 4 - j;
                                scanf("%d", &b[k][m]);
                                printf("%d\n", b[k][m]);
                        }
        }
        ```

38.   What values are printed by the following program?

```
#include <stdio.h>
void main()
{
        int x[2][4], i, j;

        for (i = 0; i < 2; i++)
                for (j = 0; j < 4; j++)
                        x[i][j] = 6;
        i = 1;
        for (j = 0; j < 2; j++)
                x[i][j] = x[j][i] + 2;
        printf("%d\n", x[i][1]);
}
```

39.   What are the values stored in the array **f** after the following statements are executed?

```
int f[4][4], i, j;
    ...
for (i = 0; i < 4; i++)
      for (j = 0; j < 4; j++)
            f[i][j] = 7;
for (i = 3; i >= 0; i--) {
      j = 0;
      while (j < 4) {
            if (i <= j)
                  f[i][j]++;
            j = j + 2;
      }
}
```

40. What is printed by the following program? Use the following data:

2 8 1 45 98 34 23 76 65 3

```
#include <stdio.h>
void main()
{
      int x[4][2], i, j;

      for (i = 0; i < 4; i++)
            for (j = 0; j < 2; j++)
                  scanf("%d", &x[i][j]);
      printf("%d\n", x[3][0]);
}
```

41. What is the value of **a[1][0]** after execution of the following segment? Use the following data: 1 2 3 4 5 6 7 8

```
int a[2][4], i, j;
    ...
for (i = 0; i < 2; i++)
      for (j = 1; j < 4; j++)
            scanf("%d", &a[i][j]);
```

42. Draw a picture of the array **test** after executing this program segment.

```
int test[4][3], i, j;
    ...
for (i = 0; i < 4; i++)
      for (j = 0; j < 3; j++)
```

```
                    test[i][j] = 1;
        for (j = 0; j < 3; j++)
                for (i = 0; i < 3; i++)
                        test[i][j] = 2;
```

43.   Write a complete C program that will

- read in a 5 × 5 array of integers, called **arr**.
- find and print the sum of all the elements of **arr**.
- find and print the product of all the elements of the third column of **arr**.
- find and print the sum of all the diagonal elements of **arr**. (The diagonal elements are **arr[0][0]**, **arr[1][1]**, **arr[2][2]**, **arr[3][3]**, and **arr[4][4]**.)

44.   What is printed by the following program segment?

```
int x[4][4], k;
   ...
x[0][0] = 5;
x[1][0] = 8;
x[2][0] = 11;
x[3][0] = -2;
for (k = 1; k < 4; k++)
        printf("%d\n", x[k][0]);
```

45.   What is printed by the following program?

```
#include <stdio.h>
void main()
{
        int y[3][4], i, j;

        for (i = 0; i < 3; i++)
                for (j  = 0; j < 4; j++) {
                        y[i][j] = 4 + 2 * i;
                        printf("%d   ", y[i][j]);
                }
        printf("\n");
        for (i = 0; i < 3; i++)
                for (j  = 0; j < 4; j++) {
                        if (i >= j)
                                y[i][j] = y[i][j] - 2;
                        printf("%d   ", y[i][j]);
                }
}
```

46.   What output will be generated by the program shown below?

```
#include <stdio.h>
void main()
{
        int intarray[2][3], i, x, y;

        i = 3;
        for (x = 0; x < 2; x++)
                for (y = 0; y < 3; y++) {
                        i = i * 2;
                        intarray[x][y] = i;
                }
        for (x = 0; x < 2; x++)
                for (y = 0; y < 3; y++) {
                        printf("%d    %d\n", x, y);
                        printf("%d\n", intarray[x][y]);
                }
        for (x = 0; x < 2; x++) {
                for (y = 0; y < 3; y++)
                        printf("%d    %d\n", x, y);
                printf("ip!  ip!  array!\n");
        }
}
```

47.   At the end of the following segment, draw a picture showing the values stored in the array
numbs.

```
int numbs[3][4], i, j;

for (i = 0; i < 3; i++)
        for (j = 0; j < 4; j++)
                numbs[i][j] = 3;
for (i = 2; i >= 0; i--)
        for (j = 0; j < 4; j++)
                if (i > j || j == 3)
                        numbs[i][j] = i + j;
                else if (i < j)
                        numbs[i][j] = -j;
```

48.   Use the following program and input file to answer both Parts (a) and (b) below. The
input file called *prob.dat* contains the numbers 1 to 16.

```
#include <stdio.h>
void main()
```

```
{
        int i, j, total, a[4][4];
        FILE * d;

        d = fopen("prob.dat", "r");
        for (j = 0; j < 4; j++)
                for (i = 0; i < 4; i++)
                        fscanf(d, "%d", &a[i][j]);
        /* Point one */
        for (i = 0; i < 4; i++)
                for (j = 0; j < 4; j++)
                        printf("%d    ", i);
        total = 0;
        for (i = 0; i < 4; i++)
                for (j = 0; j < i; j++)
                        total = total + a[i][j];
        printf("\ntotal = %d\n", total);
        fclose(d);
}
```

(a)   Draw a picture of array **a** after all the data are read in, at *Point one*.

(b)   Show exactly what will be printed.

49.   At each place where you are asked to do so, draw a picture showing the values stored in
       the array **arr** as this program executes. The data file contains the following values:

-1   2   7   -2   9   5   -4   -3   -1   0   6   8   9   -5   3   4   1   0   2   8

```
#include <stdio.h>
void main()
{
        int arr[4][3], i, j;

        for (i = 0; i < 4; i++)
                for (j = 0; j < 3; j++)
                        scanf("%d    ", &arr[i][j]);

        /* Draw a picture of the array */

        for (j = 0; j <= 2; j++)
                for (i = 0; i <= j; i++)
                        if (arr[i][j] == 0)
                                if (i == j)
                                        arr[i][j] = 25;
```

```
                                        else
                                            arr[i][j] = 0;
                              else
                                  arr[i][j] = i + j + 15;
```

/* Draw a picture of the array */

```
      }
```

50.   The portion of the a program below was written for the registrar at a college. A typical
       line of data might look like

	MALE	FRESHMAN
or	FEMALE	JUNIOR

At the place marked after the **while** loop, complete the program so that it prints the
number of males who are juniors at this college, together with an appropriate message
stating this fact.

```
      #include <stdio.h>
      #include <string.h>
      void main()
      {
            int j, k, st[4][2];
            char sex[10], status[10];

            for (k = 0; k < 4; k++)
                  for (j = 0; j < 2; j++)
                        st[k][j] = 0;
            while (scanf("%s%s", sex, status) == 2) {
                  if (strcmp(sex, "FEMALE") == 0)
                        j = 1;
                  else
                        j = 0;
                  if (strcmp(status, "FRESHMAN") == 0)
                        k = 3;
                  else if (strcmp(status, "SOPHOMORE") == 0)
                        k = 2;
                  else if (strcmp(status, "JUNIOR") == 0)
                        k = 1;
                  else
                        k = 0;
                  st[k][j]++;
      }
```

/* You are to complete this part */

}

Section 9-3   Arrays with Functions

51.   Write the function header and prototype for a function which
        (a) swaps two integer elements of an array for a sorting program.
        (b) sorts the first **n** elements of an array of integers.

52.   (a) Write a function (including comments) to perform the following tasks. The function,
        called **subsum**, will receive three parameters:

        (1) a two-dimensional array of integers called **x**, that has 3 rows and 4 columns;
        (2) an integer called **n**;
        (3) an integer called **k**.

        The function will find the sum of the **n**th row of the array **x**, and replace each element in
        the **k**th column by that sum. For example, if the function is sent an array containing the
        values below to the left (with **n = 2;** and **k = 3;**), when it returns to the main program,
        the array will contain the values below to the right. (Note: The third column is replaced by
        7's, which is the sum of the 2nd row.)

```
3  2  4  0    /* before the call */      3  2  7  0    /* after the call */
1  0  1  5                               1  0  7  5
2  1  9  3                               2  1  7  3
```

        (b) Write the C statements for a call to **subsum** from the main program; **subsum** will
        work on the third row, first column of an array called **help**. The array **help** has 3 rows
        and 4 columns of integers. Include the function prototype and variable declarations that
        are needed for the call.

53.   In the main function, you have the following declaration:

        int temps[13][7];

        Assuming that this array is filled completely, write a separate function to perform each of
        the following:

        (a) Print the entire array in a neat table.

        (b) In a single column, print all array elements that are greater than 80 or less than 10.

        (c) Print the **n**th column of the array, where **n** is an integer parameter sent to the function. The function should also print an error message if **n** is less than 0 or greater than 6.

(d) Print the table as in Part (a), but starting with the last row and proceeding in reverse order to the first.

(e) Identify the largest number stored in the array. Assume that there is only one such number.

(f) Making use of (e), print the subscripts of the element in the array in which the largest number is stored.

54. An external data file holds no more than 100 integers, with one on each line. The exact size of the file is unknown to you.

(a) Write a complete program which will read the data file into an array.

(b) Call a function which will return the average of the numbers; print it out in the main function.

(c) Call a function which will determine and print out how many of the numbers are even, how many are odd, how many are equal to or greater than the average, and how many are below the average.

You should determine the parameters for the two functions.

55. Write a function which receives two parameters: an array of integers and the number of items in the array. The function will determine the value of the largest integer and return the value to the calling program.

56. Write a function which receives three parameters: **name** which is an array of names, **age** which is an array of ages associated with the names, and **n** the number of items in the **name** and **age** arrays. Using a bubble sort, arrange the information in descending order by age. Print a table of the sorted arrays, with the name and age of the oldest person at the top. Specify all function prototypes and declarations which are needed.

57. Write a function which will receive two parameters: an array of integers whose values range from 6 to 40, and the number of items in the array. The functions should (a) count the frequency with which each value appears in the array, using an array of counters, (b) print the information computed in Part (a).

58. A theater has 30 rows, each of which has seats numbered 101-126. (a) Write an interactive program, using a two-dimensional array, which stores information about whether a ticket has been sold for any specified seat. (b) Write a function which will print the location of those seats for which a ticket has not been sold.

CHAPTER 10 - SORTING AND SEARCHING

Section 10-1   Sorting

1.   Array **num** contains the following data:

4   6   8   2   10

(a) How many passes will it take to do a *linear sort* on array **num**?

(b) How many passes will it take to do a *bubble sort* on array **num**?

2.   Write a function which will use a bubble sort to arrange an array of integers into ascending numerical order. The function will receive two parameters: the array of integers and the number of items in the array.

3.   Write a complete C program to do the following:

(a) Read an unknown number of data lines of the form:

Jones	1137	24.55
customer	four digit	amount
name	id	owed

(You can assume that the data file has a header value if you wish to use the header method.)

(b) Alphabetize the information read (by customer name) using a *bubble sort*.

(c) Print the sorted information on a page with the following heading:

CUSTOMER   ID   AMOUNT

4.   Write a complete C program (comments included) to do the following:

(a) Read a parameter value **n**, and **n** data lines, each containing a student's name and marks on 10 examinations. Print the data that is read (**n ≤ 25**).

(b) Find each student's average on the first 5 exams and then on the last 5 exams. Print these two averages.

(c) Determine for each student, if the average on the first 5 exams is equal to, greater than, or less than the average on the last 5 exams. Print a message of the result obtained.

(d) Print the number of marks that were between 80 and 89 (include both end points) for each of the 10 exams.

(e) Sort the fifth mark for each student into ascending order, carrying along the student's name. Print the names and marks that have been sorted.

(f) Print the name of the student with the second lowest mark on the fifth exam, and the name of the student with the second highest mark on the fifth exam.

Use any sorting method and indicate which is being used in a comment.

5.   The code shown below is designed to alphabetize an array of names (each name is a string of length 20). The names have already been read into an array called **name** and the number of elements read has been stored in a variable called **n**. There are several errors in the linear sort below. Circle them and show how you would correct them.

```
char name[10][20];
int i, pass, cand, n;

for (pass = 0; pass < n;  pass++)
        for (cand = pass; cand < n; cand++)
                if (strcmp(name[pass], name[cand]) > 0) {
                        strcpy(name[cand], name[pass]);
                        strcpy(name[pass], name[cand]);
                }
for (i = 0; i < n; i++)
        printf("%s\n", name[i]);
```

Section 10-2 Searching

6.   In a *linear search*, what is the purpose of the integer variable **found** in the **while** loop?

```
pos = 0;
found = FALSE;
while (pos < n && !found) {
        if (item[pos] == key){
                location = pos;
                found = TRUE;
        }
        pos++;
}
if (!found)
        location = -1;
```

7.   Rewrite the *linear search* algorithm presented in Exercise 6 eliminating the need for the variable **found**.

8.   Discuss the advantages and disadvantages of a *linear search* versus a *binary search*. Include in your discussion the necessary preparation of the array, if any. Also include the effect of the number of elements in the array on the amount of advantage. Include in your discussion the possibilities that the item searched for may not be present.

9.   Write a function which receives three parameters: an array of integers, the size of the array, and a single integer. The function will determine whether the single integer is represented in the array. You may use a *linear search* or a *binary search*. If the single integer is included in the array, return the message "yes". If it is not in the array, return "no".

10.   How many entries in the alphabetized array **pres** below will be compared to the name we are looking for, assuming we use a *linear search*? What about a *binary search*? Assume we are looking for these names:

(a)   Monroe   (c)   Eisenhower
(b)   Truman   (d)   Washington

pres

0	Adams
1	Eisenhower
2	Ford
3	Grant
4	Johnson
5	Kennedy
6	Lincoln
7	Monroe
8	Nixon
9	Washington

CHAPTER 11 - STRING MANIPULATION IN C

In this chapter, show blanks where necessary with a b̸ (b with a slash through it.)

Section 11-1 String Representation

1.	Describe how strings are represented in C.

2.	What is the result of the following program?

```
#include <stdio.h>
void main()
{
        char word1[20] = "Horton Hears a";
        char word2[20] = {'W', 'h', 'o', '\0'};

        printf("%s  %s\n", word1, word2);
}
```

3.	What is the result of executing the following program? Assume a data file *datain.dat*, which consists of the following two lines:

```
The Cat
In the Hat Comes Back!
```

```
#include <stdio.h>
void main()
{
        char word1[10], word2[10], sentence[80];
        int c, i;
        FILE * datafile;

        datafile = fopen("datain.dat", "r");
        fscanf(datafile, "%s%s", word1, word2);
        i = 0;
        while ((c = fgetc(datafile)) != EOF && i < 79) {
                sentence[i] = c;
                i++;
        }
        sentence[i] = '\0';

        printf("%s %s  %s\n", word1, word2, sentence);
```

- 150 -

```
        }
```

4.   In Exercise 3, two methods were used to read the strings from the data file. Explain the
        advantages and disadvantages of using **scanf** rather than **fgetc**?

5.   What is the result of the following program? Use the data below:

1111	Donald	Duck	35.0
2222	Mickey	Mouse	42.5
3333	Betty	Boop	28.2

```
#include <stdio.h>
void main()
{
        char first[10], last[10];
        int i = 0, id;
        float age, total = 0.0;

        while (scanf("%d%s%s%f", &id, first, last, &age) == 4) {
                total = total + age;
                i++;
                printf("%s, %s is %4.1f years old\n", last, first, age);
        }
        printf("\nThe average age is %4.1f\n", total / i);
}
```

6.   Describe why the address operator (**&**) is used in Exercise 5 when reading the variable **id**
        and **age**, but not when reading the variables **first** and **last**?

7.   Write a function **getline** that reads up to 80 characters from *stdin* and returns a C string
        to the calling program. The function should terminate reading upon encountering the **eof**
        or the '\n' character.

8.   Write a function which returns the length of a string which is passed to it as a parameter.

9.   Show exactly what is printed by the following program:

```
#include <stdio.h>
void main()
{
        char word[25] = "Computer";
        int i, j;

        i = 0;
```

```
            while (word[i] != '\0') {
                    for (j = 0; j < i; j++)
                            printf(" ");
                    printf("%c\n", word[i++]);
            }
            i--;
            while (i >= 0) {
                    for (j = i-1; j >= 0; j--)
                            printf(" ");
                    printf("%c\n", word[i--]);
            }
    }
```

10.   What is printed by the following program? Use the following data:

       She Sells Sea Shells At The Sea Shore.

```
#include <stdio.h>
#include <ctype.h>
void main()
{
        char line[80], c;
        int i;
        void word(char *);

        i = 0;
        while ((c = getchar()) != EOF && i < 79) {
                line[i] = c;
                i++;
        }
        line[i] = '\0';
        word(line);
}

void word(char *p)
{
        while (*p != '\0') {
                if (*p == ' ')
                        putchar('\n');
                else
                        putchar(toupper(*p));
                p++;
        }
}
```

Section 11-2   The *string.h* library

11.   State what is printed by each of the following program segments. Use these declarations and initial values for each part:

```
char str1[40] = "ABCDE12345", str[40];
char *p;
int i = 3, j;
```

(a)
```
strcpy(str, str1);
printf("%s\n", str);
```

(b)
```
p = str1 + 5;
strcpy(str, p);
printf("%s\n", str);
```

(c)
```
p = str ;
for (j = 5; j < 8; j++)
        *p++ = str1[j];
*p='\0';
printf("%s\n", str);
```

(d)
```
p = str ;
for (j = 5; j < strlen(str1); j++)
        *p++ = str1[j];
*p='\0';
printf("%s\n", str);
```

(e)
```
p = str ;
for (j = i; j < strlen(str1)-2; j++)
        *p++ = str1[j];
*p='\0';
printf("%s\n", str);
```

12.   Which of the following program segments *may* cause an error? Describe the circumstances which will cause the error, if any. Use the following declarations:

```
char str1[10] = "COMPUTER", str2[20] = "INFORMATION SCIENCE";
char *p;
int i;
```

(a)   `strcat(str2, "s");`

(b)   `strcpy(str2, str1);`

     (c)   p = str1;
               strcpy(str2, p + 5);

     (d)   p = str2;
               strcpy(str1, p + 5);

     (e)   strcpy(str1, str2 + 15);

     (e)   strcpy(str2, str1+ 2);

13.   What will be printed by execution of the following program segment (which highlights similarities and differences in the use of the *blank* and *null* strings)?

```
char word1[10], word2[10], blank[10] = " ", null[10] = "";
int len;

strcpy(word1, "ALPHA");
strcpy(word2, "ALPHA  ");
if (strcmp(word1, word2) == 0)
        printf("Blanks at the end don't count.\n");
else
        printf("Blanks at the end do count.\n");
if (strlen(word1) == strlen(word2))
        printf("A blank is a null string.\n");
else
        printf("%s\n%s\n%s\n",
                "A blank is not a null string",
                "The blank within quotes is",
                "A legal character");
strcat(word1, null);
/* What is the effect of the above statement? */
len = strlen(word1);
printf("%d\n", len);
strcat(word1, blank);
len = strlen(word1);
printf("%d\n", len);
printf("%s%s\n", null, "A blank and a null string are different");
printf("%s%s\n", blank, "A blank and a null string are different");
```

14.   Write a function, called **reverse**, which receives as a parameter a string and which returns the string with the characters in the opposite order. For example, if the string "ABC" were sent as a parameter, "CBA" would be returned.

15.   (a) Assume **code** is an integer variable containing a value which is between 3 and 5

digits long. Write the C declaration and statement(s) needed to print the next to last digit (from the right). For example, if **code** is 4327, we want to print 2.

(b) Assume **code** is a string variable which is between 3 and 5 characters long. Write the C declarations and statement(s) needed to print the next to last character (from the right). For example, if **code** is "MARK" then we want to print "R".

16.   What will be printed by each of the following statements?

```
char str[20] = "ABC123";
```

(a)   printf("%s\n", strstr("ABCBA", "A"));

(b)   printf("%s\n", strstr("A", "ABCBA"));

(c)   printf("%s\n", strstr("BBBAA", "AA"));

(d)   printf("%s\n", strstr("ABCBA", "BA"));

(e)   printf("%s\n", strstr(str, "str"));

(f)   printf("%s\n", strstr("ABC ABC", " A"));

(g)   printf("%s\n", strstr("4ABC123123", str));

(h)   printf("%s\n", strstr("4ABC123123", "str"));

17.   Show exactly what is printed by the following program:

```
#include <stdio.h>
#include <string.h>
void main()
{
        char   first[15] = "Monticello",
               last[10] = "NY",
               middle[20] = "Liberty";
        char   one = 'H';
        int    k, m;

        k = strlen(middle);
        m = sizeof(first);
        printf("%d   %d\n", k, m);

        strcat(middle, last);
        strcpy(last, "Fallsburg");
```

```
            first[11] = 'N';
            first[12] = 'Y';
            first[13] = '\0';
            printf("%s   %s    %s\n", first, middle, last);

            if (strcmp(first, middle) > 0)
                    printf("bigger\n");
            else
                    printf("smaller\n");

            *(middle + 4) = one;
            middle[5]++;
            printf("%s\n", middle);
    }
```

18.   For each of the *string.h* library functions— **strcat**, **strcmp**, **strcpy**, **strlen**, and
      strstr— state whether the function returns a value of type **char ***, **int**, or **void**. Also, tell
      how many parameters each function takes and the data type of each of the parameters.

19.   Show exactly what is printed by the following program:

```
        #include <stdio.h>
        #include <string.h>
        void main()
        {
            char    eight[8] = "TUVWXYZ",
                    nine[9] = "LMNOP",
                    twenty[20] = "twenty";
            int     j, k;

            strcpy(twenty, nine);
            strcat(twenty, eight);
            printf("%s   %s     %s\n", eight, nine, twenty);

            if (strcmp(nine, twenty) > 0)
                    k = strlen(nine) * sizeof(twenty) + strlen(twenty);
            else
                    k = strlen(twenty) + 5 * sizeof(eight);
            printf("%d\n", k);

            eight[2] = '\n';
            eight[3]++;
            eight[4]--;
            eight[5]='\0';
```

```
            eight[6] = 'Q';
            printf("%s\n", eight);
            for (j = 0; j <= 6; j++)
                    printf("%c", eight[j]);
            printf("\n");
    }
```

20.   What is printed by the following program?

```
        #include <stdio.h>
        #include <string.h>
        void main()
        {
                char stringarray[10][20], str[11], temp[20];
                int i;

                strcpy(str, "AAAAA");
                strcpy(stringarray[0], "b");
                for (i = 0; i < 9; i++) {
                        strcpy(temp,"a");
                        strcat(temp, stringarray[i]);
                        strcat(temp, "A");
                        strcpy(stringarray[i+1], temp);
                        printf("%s   %d\n", stringarray[i],strlen(stringarray[i]));
                }
                stringarray[2][1] = 'z';
                printf("%s\n", stringarray[3]);
                str[1] = 'z';
                printf("%s\n", str);
        }
```

CHAPTER 12 - STRUCTURES

Section 12.1 Structure Variables

1.   How many memory locations (members) are reserved by each of the following:

    (a)   **struct** {
                 char ssno[9];
                 char last[20], first[20], mi;
                 int code, credits;
                 char course[10];
             } student1, student2;

    (b)   **struct** {
                 char ssno[9];
                 char last[20], first[20], mi;
                 int code[5], credits[5];
                 char course[5][10];
             } student1, student2;

    (c)   **struct** student {
                 char ssno[9];
                 char last[20], first[20], mi;
                 int code[5], credits[5];
                 char course[5][10];
             };

    (d)   **struct** student {
                 char ssno[9];
                 char last[20], first[20], mi;
                 int code[5], credits[5];
                 char course[5][10];
             };
             struct student st[100];

2.   Distinguish between a *tag name* and a *structure variable*.

3.   What will be printed by the following program? Use the following data:

             Barbara   10.50   35.0

             #include <stdio.h>

```
void main()
{
        struct {
                char name[20];
                float rate, hours, pay;
        } worker;

        scanf("%s%f%f", worker.name, &worker.rate, &worker.hours);
        worker.pay = worker.rate * worker.hours;
        printf("%.2f\n", worker.pay);
}
```

4. Write a **scanf** statement that will print the value of breakfast's liquid, lunch's liquid, and supper's solids given the following declaration:

```
struct meal {
        char solid[5];
        int liquid;
};

struct {
        struct meal breakfast, lunch, supper;
} diet;
```

5. Declare a structure which might be used to store information about a book consisting of title, author, publisher, catalog number, year of publication, number of pages, and price.

6. Declare a structure to store information about a student. The structure should hold the following pieces of information:

*   the student's name consisting of a last name, first name, and middle initial,
*   the student's birthdate consisting of a month, day, and year,
*   the student's grade point average (this is a real number),
*   the student's id (a 4-digit number),
*   the student's expected date of graduation, and
*   the student's major

7. Declare a structure to store information about three brands of cars: Ford, Chevrolet, and Toyota. For each brand we wish to store the following pieces of information:

*   price
*   year
*   model
*   cylinders
*   horsepower

- color

8.   We want to use a structure to store information about a student. The structure should hold the following pieces of information for the student:
   - the student's name, consisting of a first and last name (each of which is up to 15 characters).
   - the student's class-and-curriculum number (a 3-digit integer).
   - the student's grades on five exams (each of which is an integer).
   - the student's average (this is a real number), and
   - the student's letter grade in the course (e.g., 'A' or 'B').

   (a) Give the declaration for such a structure.

   (b) Read in the first name and class-and-curriculum number for the student.

   (c) Write a function which will compute the average of the five grades and store it in the structure.

   (d) Write a function which assigns the proper letter grade based upon the student's average. (Use the usual rules. e.g., 'A': $90 \leq$ average ≤ 100; 'B': $80 \leq$ average < 90, etc.)

   (e) Determine if the student satisfies both of the following rules: "the class-and-curriculum number is 600 or more and the letter grade is 'F'". If the students does satisfy both rules, print the student's entire name. If not, print a message saying "NO GOOD".

Section 12.2 - Array of Structures

9.   What will be printed by the following program? Use the following sets of data:

Sarah	NY	5.50	25.00
Mary	FL	9.50	35.00
Bill	CA	8.00	20.00

```
#include <stdio.h>
void main()
{
        struct wages {
                float rate, hours, pay;
        };

        struct location {
                char street[15], city[10], state[3], zip[6];
        };
```

```
struct {
        char name[20];
        struct location address;
        struct wages payroll;
} worker[3];

int i;
float sum;

for (i = 0; i < 3; i++) {
        scanf("%s%s%f%f",
                worker[i].name,
                worker[i].address.state,
                &worker[i].payroll.rate,
                &worker[i].payroll.hours);
        worker[i].payroll.pay = worker[i].payroll.hours *
                                        worker[i].payroll.rate;
        sum  = sum + worker[i].payroll.pay;
        printf("%s  %.2f  %s\n",
                worker[i].name,
                worker[i].payroll.pay,
                worker[i].address.state);
}
printf("Total salary paid was %.2f\n", sum);
}
```

10.   Given the following structure:

```
struct army {
        char general[20];
        struct {
                char colonel[20];
                struct  {
                        char captain[20];
                        int soldiers;
                } company[10];
        } regiment[5];
} division [10];
```

(a) Write C statements that will print out the name of the captain of the last company of the fourth regiment of the first division.

(b) Write a C statement(s) that will move the contents of the entire fifth regiment of the third division to the third regiment of the sixth division.

(c) Write a C statement(s) needed to print out the names of all the generals in the army.

11.   Given the following declarations:

```
struct info {
        char birthday[6];
        char haircolor[10];
}

struct info father, mother, siblings[5];
```

Write the C statement(s) needed to print the hair color of the father, and the birthday of the third sibling.

12.   Each of the following questions refers to the structure shown below:

(a) Write a program segment to print the names of the first three daughters of the second family (or as many daughters as they have, if they do not have three).

(b) Write a program segment to sort and then list the children of the seventh family alphabetically by first name.

(c) Write a program segment to print the number of mothers who have maiden names the same as their husband's last name.

(d) Write a program segment to print the father's name and the address of any family living in zip code 11210.

(e) Write a statement to print the first name of the second child of the third family.

(f) Write the identifier necessary to access the first name of the third child of the second family.

```
struct person {
        char first[15], last[15], mi;
        int age;
};

struct location {
        char street[25], city[10], state[3], zip[6];
};

struct relations{
        struct person father;
```

```
                struct {
                        struct person name;
                        char maiden[15];
                } mother;
                int no_of_children;
                struct kid {
                        struct person name;
                        char gender[6];
                } child[5];
                struct location address;
        } family[10];
```

13. Write a program to do the following:

    (a) Read an unknown number of student records (maximum 100) including name, which consists of last, first, and middle; address, which consists of street address, city, state, and zip code; and courses (up to 6 each), which consists of codes and credits.

    (b) Sort the records in increasing order of zip code.

    (c) Print the records in the newly sorted order.

14. Data about a company's employees are stored using the structure shown below. Write a program segment to print names and addresses of all employees who live in zip code 11210. Assume that the data are already in memory.

```
        struct location {
                char street[15], city[15], state[3], zip[6];
        };

        struct person {
                char last[15], first[15], mi;
        };

        struct {
                char ss_no[10];
                struct person name;
                struct location address;
        } empl[100];
```

15. An instructor is teaching two sections of an introductory programming course, with 35 students in each section. The instructor uses two structure variables to keep track of student performance. Assume that data have already been read into the structures.

```
        struct person {
```

```
                    char last[20], first[20];
            };

            struct marks {
                    float quiz1, quiz2, midterm, final;
            };

            struct section {
                    struct person name;
                    struct marks grade;
            } section1[35], section2[35];
```

(a) Print a list of complete names of all the students in Section 2.

(b) Compute the average midterm grade for all students in Section 1.

(c) Write a function which prints the name of the student with the highest grade on the final. The student can be from either section. Assume that there is only one student with the highest grade. Also print the student's section.

(d) Write a function which compares the scores of the first student in each class on the midterm and on the final. Print a message to tell if the same student scored better on both, or if they each scored better on one of these exams. Print an appropriate message if they tied on either exam.

16.   Use the following array of structures to answer the questions below.

```
            struct person {
                    char first[15], last[15];
            };

            struct points {
                    int last_term, present_term, total;
            };

            struct index {
                    float last_term, present_term, overall;
            };

            struct {
                    struct person name;
                    struct points credits;
                    struct index gpa;
            } student[MAXSTUDENTS];
```

(a) Write a C statement to print the last name, total number of credits, and overall index of the 25th student.

(b) Write a C statement(s) to read the first name, last name, last term's index, and this term's index for the first and 50th students.

(c) Write C statement(s) to set last term's credits and index equal to this term's credit and index, respectively, for every student.

17.   Consider the following structure:

```
struct {
        char name[20];
        int age;
        float hours_worked[7], rate, pay;
} employee[10];
```

(a) What is the total number of values that can be stored in this structure?

(b) Write a statement to set the 6th employee's rate to 25.50.

(c) Write the series of statements which sets each employee's PAY to the RATE times the total number of hours worked for the week.

18.   Assume that we have two structures declared to keep track of the 10 cars owned by two rental companies. Assume that the data have already been read into the structures.

```
struct odometer {
        float starting, ending;
};

struct cars {
        char modelname[9];
        float rate;
        int daysout;
        struct odometer miles;
} hertzcar[10], aviscar[10];
```

For each of the following parts, write a series of C statements (or functions) to accomplish the required task:

(a) Print the complete structure for the AVIS car with the longest trip (the largest difference between the starting and ending mileage).

(b) Print the average rate for the group of all HERTZ cars, and also the average rate for the group of all AVIS cars.

(c) Print the model name of each HERTZ car that was out for more than **7 days**.

(d) Print the model names of all AVIS cars for which the rate is greater than **15.37**.

(e) Print the number of days out for each car which has CHRYSLER as its model name. Do this for both companies, HERTZ and AVIS.

19.   Given the structure

```
struct {
        char manager[20];
        struct {
                int quantity;
                float price;
        } coffee_sold;
        struct {
                int quantity;
                float price;
        } cake_sold;
} stores[50];
```

(a) Write the C statement that will make the quantity of coffee sold at store 24 equal to the sum of the quantity of coffee sold at the first and last stores.

(b) Write the C statement(s) which will print
   (i)   the name of the manager of the third store.
   (ii) the price of cake at the first store.
   (iii) the price of cake at the tenth store.
   (iv) the price of coffee at the eleventh store.
   (v)   the total receipts (quantity times price) of each of the stores.

Note: An entire structure, an array of structures, or an individual member can be sent as a parameter (either *by value* or by the use of pointers) to a function.

20.   Using the structure declared in Exercise 10, write the function invocation, the function prototype, and the function header of a function **func** of type **void** that will receive as a parameter from the calling function:
(a) the entire structure.
(b) the information about **division[9]**.
(c) the information about the third regiment of the seventh division.

21.   Using the structure declared in Exercise 12, write the function invocation, the function prototype, and the function header of a function **func** of type **void** to process

(a) the entire structure.
(b) the information about **family[9]**.

22. Using the structure declared in Exercise 15, write the function invocation, the function
prototype, and the function header of a function **func** to process
(a) the entire structure for both sections.
(b) the final grades of Section 1.

23. Use the structure declared in Exercise 12 as the structure of the calling function for this
exercise. Write a function invocation statement as well as a function to print (from the
function) the number of children in each family which have surnames different from the
surname of the father.

24. Consider the following structure declaration:

```
struct book {
        char authorname[15];
        int subject[3];
        int bookcode, pages;
} library[100];
```

(a) Write one or more statements to print the code and the author's name for book
number 43 in the library.

(b) Print all three subjects for book 6 and 7.

(c) Suppose we want to know how many books in the library have at least 250 pages.
Write a function to print this number. If there are no books with at least 250 pages, the
function should print the word "NONE".

(d) Write a function which will return a pointer to an array which contains the names of all
authors who have written a book one of whose subject codes is "9".

25. We want to use a structure to store information about up to twenty-five students. The
structure should hold the following pieces of information for each student:
• the student's name, consisting of a first and last name (each of which is up to 15
characters).
• the student's class-and-curriculum number (a 3-digit integer).
• the student's grades on five exams (each of which is an integer).
• the student's average (this is a real number), and
• the student's letter grade in the course (e.g., 'A' or 'B').

(a) Give the declaration for such a structure.

(b) Read in the first name and class-and-curriculum number for each of the students.

(Note: we do not know in advance how many students there are.)

(c) Write a function which will, for each student, compute the average of the five grades and store it in the structure.

(d) Write a function which assigns the proper letter grade to each student based upon the student's average. (Use the usual rules. e.g., 'A': $90 \leq average \leq 100$; 'B': $80 \leq average < 90$, etc.)

(e) Write a function which will print the entire name of each student who satisfies both of the following rules: "the class-and-curriculum number is 600 or more and the letter grade is 'F'".

Section 12-3   Structures with Functions

26.   (a) Declare a structure which will contain the following information about a student:

- First name - at most 10 characters
- Last name - at most 15 characters
- Social Security Number - 9 characters
- GPA - real number
- Curriculum number - integer
- An array of 5 numeric grades

(b) Write a function **printinfo**, which will accept a pointer to a structure defined as above, and will print the information in a pretty manner.

(c) Give the declaration for an entire class, where the class is made up of at most 30 students.

(d) Modify the function of Part (b) so that it will accept a pointer to a structure and an integer, representing the number of students in the class, and will print the information of all the students on the class in a pretty manner.

27.   Given a structure containing an employee's name, rate of pay, and number of hours worked, write a function which returns the individual's pay.

28.   Given a structure as shown below which contains a student's grades, write a function which returns the student's average and letter grade. The average is to be computed as 30% of the midterm + 30% of the final + 40% of the homeworks; with the letter grade assigned in the usual fashion (e.g., A: ≥ 90; B: ≥ 80; C ≥ 70; etc.).

```
struct student {
    char first[10], last10];
```

```
                int midterm, final, homework[5];
                float average;
                char grade;
        }
```

29.   Given an array of structures containing first and last names and the number of items in the array, write a function which sorts the array by last name.

30.   Given an array of structures containing names and phone numbers and the number of data sets in the array, write a function that returns the name associated with a particular phone number.

31.   Given an array of student structures containing names, student id's, and grades, write functions to:
        (a) sort the array by grade
        (b) given a student id, search for and return that student's name and grade.

CHAPTER 13 - NUMBER SYSTEMS

Section 13.1   Decimal

1.   (a) What is the value of 10^2? 10^1? 10^0?

(b) In terms of positional notation, explain why the number 123 is different from the number 321.

2.   Devise a C statement, which will convert a variable **ch** (of type **char**) containing a digit to its decimal equivalent. For example, the statement will yield the value 9 from the character '9' , or 0 from '0'.

3.   Devise a C statement, which will convert a decimal digit to the equivalent character. For example, 9 would yield '9' and 0 would yield '0'.

4.   Write a function **convert** which will accept a string of length 3 containing digits only, and will return the decimal equivalent. For example, if the string '987' is passed to the function, the function will return 987. (Hint: see Exercise 2.)

5.   Define a function **dstring** which will accept a 3 digit integer and return the equivalent string. For example, if 987 is passed to the function, it will return '987'. (Hint: see Exercise 3.)

Section 11-2   Binary and Hexadecimal

6.   Count the number of your fingers using the binary number system (with binary digits 0 and 1 only).

7.   Count the number of your fingers and toes using the hexadecimal number system.

8.   How many binary digits (bits) does it take to count from zero to nine? From zero to fifteen?

9.   State exactly what each of the bits in the binary number 111 represents.

10.   (a) State exactly what each of the digits in the hexadecimal number 0x111 represents.
(b) Repeat the process for the number 0x9A0.

11.   Convert each of the following decimal numbers to binary:

(a) 201   (b) 256   (c) 94   (d) 10   (e) 1000

12.   Convert each of the following hexadecimal numbers to binary:

   (a) 0x201   (b) 0x256   (c) 0x94   (d) 0x10   (e) 0x1000
   (f) 0xDAD   (g) 0xDC10 (h) 0xC0B (i) 0xABC

13.   Convert each of the following decimal numbers to hexadecimal:

   (a) 500   (b) 707   (c) 18   (d) 1111   (e) 1232

14.   Convert each of the following binary numbers to decimal:

   (a) 1101   (b) 100   (c) 1010   (d) 0101
   (e) 1100101   (f) 100010101   (g) 1110001   (h) 1010101010
   (i) 100100   (j) 1100110   (k) 1000001   (l) 111111100

15.   Convert each of the binary numbers of Exercise 14 to hexadecimal.

16.   Distinguish between the numbers 10, 010, and 0x10.

17.   Do the following conversions. Show all work.

   (a) $(152)_{10}$ to base 8

   (b) $(284)_{16}$ to base 2

   (c) $(11010101)_2$ to base 10

18.   Perform the following in binary and check your results using decimal.

   (a)   110011   (b)   111000
          + 1111   +10000
          ‾‾‾‾‾‾‾   ‾‾‾‾‾‾‾

   (c)   100010   (d)   101010
          × 1001   × 1111
          ‾‾‾‾‾‾‾   ‾‾‾‾‾‾‾

FINAL EXAMINATION 1

Part I 60 pts (6 questions, 10 points each)

1.   Show what is printed by the following program. If a storage location has not been
        assigned a value, use **??** when asked to print its value.

```c
#include <stdio.h>

void main()
{
    int arr[10];
    int j, k;

    for (j = 2; j <= 8; j++)
        arr[j] = 10 * j;

    for (k = 0; k <= 9; k++)  {
        if (k == 1)
                continue;
        printf(" %d ", arr[k]);
        if (k == 8)
                break;
    }
    printf("\n\n");

    arr[7] += 100;
    arr[4]++;
    arr[0] = 3;
    arr[1] = 0;
    arr[9] = 1;
    arr[3] = arr[2] * 2;

    for (k = 0; k <= 9; k++)
        printf(" %d ", arr[k]);
    printf("\n\n");

    for (j = 0; j <= 8; j += 2)
        if (arr[j] < arr[j+1])
                arr[j]++;
        else
```

```
                    arr[j] = -2;

            for (k = 0; k <= 9; k++)
                    printf(" %d ", arr[k]);
            printf("\n\n");
    }
```

2.   Show what is printed by the program shown below.

```
#include <stdio.h>

void change(int *, int *, int);
int answer(int, int);

void main()
{
        int a = 20, b = 7, c = 5;
        int result;

        result = answer(a, b);
        printf("%d %d %d %d\n", result, a, b, c);

        change(&a, &b, c);
        printf("%d %d %d\n",a, b, c);

        a = 1;
        b = 8;
        c = 6;
        change(&a, &b, c);
        printf("%d %d %d\n", a, b, c);
}

void change(int *a, int *b, int c)
{
        *a += 4;
        c--;
        if (*a > *b)
                if (*b < c)
                        *a = 15;
                else
                        *b = 100;
        else
                c += 1000;
        printf("in change %d %d %d\n", *a, *b, c);
        return;
```

```
        }

        int answer(int x, int y)
        {
                int c, d;

                c = x / y + 3;
                d = x % (y + 3);
                printf("c is %d, d is %d\n", c, d);
                if (c > d)
                        return c;
                else
                        return d;
        }
```

3.   (a) Show exactly what will be printed by the program shown below, assuming that 5 and 1 are typed in as data.

```
        #include <stdio.h>

        void main()
        {
                int a, b;

                scanf("%d", &a);
                scanf("%d", &b);
                while (a >= 0) {
                        a += b;
                        b -= 7;
                        printf("%d %d\n", a, b);
                }
                printf("outside %d %d\n", a, b);
        }
```

(b) Answer Part (a) again, assuming that the values -1 and 3 are typed in as data.

(c) Answer Part (a) again, assuming that the values 6 and 4 are typed in as data.

4.   Show exactly what is printed by the following program.

```
        #include <stdio.h>
        #include <string.h>
```

```
void main()
{
        char six[6] = "HIJK";
        char seven[7] = "ABCDE";
        char ten[10] = "ten";
        int m, k;

        strcpy(ten, seven);
        strcat(ten, six);
        printf("%s %s\n%s\n", six, seven, ten);

        if (strcmp(six, seven) > 0)
                printf("case 1\n");
        else
                printf("case 2\n");

        k = strlen(six) + 10 * strlen(seven);

        printf("%d\n",k);

        seven[2] = '\n';
        seven[3]++;
        seven[4] = 'Q';
        seven[5] = '\0';
        seven[6] = 'f';

        printf("%s\n", seven);

        for (m = 0; m <= 6; m++)
                printf("%c", seven[m]);
        printf("\n");
}
```

5.   (a) Show what is printed by the following program.

```
#include <stdio.h>

void main()
{
        int x = 3, y = 30, z = 5;

        if ( y != 7  &&  x + y <= z)
                printf("alpha\n");
```

```
                    else
                          if (y - x < 4  ||  z >= 4)
                                  printf("beta\n");
                          else
                                  printf("gamma\n");
                    printf("delta\n");
              }
```

(b) Repeat part a assuming that the variables have these initial values:

        x = 1;   y = 1;   z = 5;

(c) Repeat part a for these values:

        x = 2;   y = 7;   z = 1;

6.   (a) Write a function **changetoavg** to do the following:

The function will have two parameters:
      numbs — an array of doubles
      n — an integer from 1 to 100, giving the number of values actually in
            the **numbs** array

The function will determine the average of the first **n** elements in the numbs array. It will print this average. Then the function will set each of the first **n** elements in the array to the value computed for the average.

For example, assume that **n** is 4 and the array holds 5.0 -7.0 3.0 6.0. The function will print a message saying the average is 1.75; each of the first 4 elements will be changed to this value. The new array will hold these values: 1.75 1.75 1.75 1.75.

(b) Assume that the main program wants the function to modify the first 20 elements in an array called **xyz**.

Give the call to the function from a main program.

When the function returns, the main program should print the new values in the array.

Give the function prototype.

Assume that the array **xyz** will hold no more than 100 doubles. Give the declaration for all variables used in the call from the main program to the function and in printing the new values.

This question is optional. You do not have to answer it. If you do answer part or all of it correctly, you will get extra credit.

7.   We want to use a structure to store information about a student. The structure should hold the following pieces of information for the student:

- the student's name (the name is divided into two parts: a first name and a last name, each of which is up to 15 characters),

- the student's class-and-curriculum number (a 3-digit integer),

- the student's grades on four exams (each is an integer),

- the student's average (this is a real number), and

- the student's letter grade in the course (e.g., 'A' or 'C').

(a) Give a declaration for such a structure.

Use your declaration from Part (a) for the remaining parts. For each of the following, give one or more C statements which will accomplish what is requested.

(b) Read in the first name and class-and-curriculum number for the student.

(c) Compute the average of the four exam grades and store it in the structure.

(d) Determine if the student satisfies both of the following rules: the class-and-curriculum number is 600 or more and the letter grade is 'F'. If the student does satisfy both rules, print the student's entire name. If not, print a message saying "No good."

Part II Short answer questions   15 pts

A.   Base systems and conversions (6 pts):

     (a) Convert 1001010 (base 2) to base 10   Answer: _____

     (b) Convert 59 (base 10) to base 2   Answer: _____

     (c) Assume that you have a number which is represented using 3 hexadecimal symbols (e.g., FA9 or 46E). What is the largest number of bits that will be required to represent this hexadecimal number?

(d) Perform the following addition of two binary (base 2) numbers. Your answer should be a number in binary.

$$1001 + 1011 = ?$$

(e) What is the largest number that can be represented in base 2 using 6 bits?

(1) Show the number in base 2.

(2) Show the corresponding base 16 representation of the number.

B.   For each of the following, select the letter of the best choice (9 pts).

1.   Which of the following is an example of a compilation error?
      a. forgetting to initialize a variable to 0
      b. forgetting to include comments for a program
      c. forgetting to declare a variable
      d. using **2 * x** instead of **3 * x** in a formula
      e. reading 3.5 as the data value for a variable of type **int**

                                                        1 ans. _____

2.   What is the name of the process which involves determining what is wrong with a program and correcting the mistakes?
      a. documentation
      b. pseudocode
      c. flowcharting
      d. problem-solving
      e. debugging

                                                        2 ans. _____

3.   Turbo C is which of the following:
      a. the name of the personal computer on which we run programs
      b. a piece of hardware used for input of programs
      c. a piece of software used to edit, compile, and run programs
      d. the operating system used to control the personal computer
      e. the menu displayed when you first turn the computer on

                                                        3 ans. _____

4. Two major differences between a hard disk and a floppy are:
   a. the hard disk can store more information and the floppy is usually more reliable
   b. the floppy can store more information and the floppy is usually more reliable
   c. the hard disk is more reliable and the floppy can store more information
   d. the hard disk can store more information and the floppy can be moved from one place to another
   e. the floppy can store more information and the hard disk can be moved from one place to another

   4 ans. _____

5. Structured programming encourages all of the following except:
   a. using functions or modules
   b. avoiding the use of data type double
   c. indenting and aligning in a program
   d. using mnemonic names for variables
   e. including comments in a program

   5 ans. _____

6. A system in which several computers are connected is said to form a:
   a. modem
   b. network
   c. mainframe computer
   d. parallel computer
   e. database machine

   6 ans. _____

7. Which of the following is an example of an execution error?
   a. forgetting to include comments for a program
   b. forgetting to declare a variable
   c. using **2 * y** instead of **3 * y** in a formula
   d. reading in 3 as the data value for a variable of type **double**
   e. dividing by a variable whose value is 0

   7 ans. _____

8. Bit, byte, and word are terms used to describe:
   a. software
   b. an operating system
   c. a compiler
   d. memory
   e. a printer

   8 ans. _____

9.   Which of the following allows a person using one computer to access information stored
        on a computer located somewhere else?
        a. a modem
        b. a CD-ROM drive
        c. a hard disk
        d. a printer
        e. a monitor

                                                                    9 ans. _____

Part III (25 pts)

Write a complete program that will process a list of names and grade point averages (GPA).
There are a maximum 100 names on the list. The GPA's range from 0.00 to 4.00.

The data values are arranged as follows:

   •   The first line contains a parameter, **n**, which is the actual number of names (with
        GPA's) in the list.

   •   The next N lines each contain a name and a GPA, with the name consisting of a first
        name (maximum of 15 characters) followed by one or more blanks, followed by the
        last name(maximum of 15 characters). For example:

                George Washington   3.85

Your program should do the following:

(a)   Read the data and store it in an appropriate array(s) or structure. The name should be
        separated into a first name and a last name to meet the requirements of the report
        specified below.

(b)   Call a function to sort the data in decreasing numerical order by GPA.

(c)   Print a table of names and corresponding GPA's. The student with the highest GPA is
        printed first, and the student with the lowest GPA is printed last. The data should be
        printed out with the last name beginning in column 10, followed by a comma and a blank
        and then the first name. The GPA is printed following the name.

(d)   Use a function to calculate the mean (average) GPA, and print this result, properly
        identified, several lines below the end of the table.

FINAL EXAMINATION 2

Part I 63 points   (questions 1-5, 9 points each; question 6, 12 pts; question 7, 6 pts)

1. At each place where it is requested, draw a picture showing the values stored in the array **arr**.

```c
#include <stdio.h>

void main()
{
        int arr[8];
        int i;

        for (i = 0; i < 8; i++)
                arr[i] = 100 + i;

        /*  draw the array here */

        arr[5] = 104;
        arr[3] = 35;
        arr[1] = 200;
        arr[6] = 110;

        /*  draw the array here */

        for (i = 1; i < 7; i++)
                if (arr[i] > arr[i + 1])
                        arr[i] = arr[i] + 1000;
                else if (arr[i] == arr[i + 1])
                                arr[i] *= 10;
                else arr[i] = -7;

        /*  draw the array here */

}
```

2. Show exactly what is printed by the following program.

```c
#include <stdio.h>
#include <string.h>
void main()
```

```
{
        char   first[12] = "Washington",
               last[10] = "X",
               final[20] = "Georgie";
        char one = 'H';
        int k, m;

        k = strlen(final);
        m = sizeof(first);
        printf("%d %d\n\n", k, m);

        strcat(final, last);
        strcpy(last, "Adams");
        first[5] = 'Y';
        printf("%s %s %s\n", first, last, final);

        if (strcmp(first, final) > 0)
                printf("bigger\n");
        else
                printf("smaller\n");

        *(final+2) = one;
        (*(final+4))++;
        printf("%s\n",final);
}
```

3.   (a) Show what is printed by the following program.

```
#include <stdio.h>
void changes(int *x, int *y, int z);

void main()
{
        int a = 6, b = 15, c = 100;

        changes(&a, &b, c);
        printf("In main: %d %d %d \n", a, b, c);

        a = 6;  b = 15;  c = 100;
        changes(&c, &a, b);
        printf("In main: %d %d %d \n", a, b, c);
}

void changes(int *x, int *y, int z)
```

```
{
        int a = 99;

        if (*x < *y) {
                *y = *x - 1;
                *x = -1;
        }
        else {
                *y = 1000;
                *x -= 5;
        }
        z++;
        printf("In changes: %d %d %d\n", *x, *y, z);
}
```

(b) Consider each of the following calls to the function changes. For each one, decide whether or not it is valid. In one sentence (NO MORE!), justify your answer.

i. changes(*a, &b, c);

ii. changes(&a, &b, c+1);

4.   Show exactly what is printed by Parts (a) and (b) Assume that all variables used in this question have the data type **int**.

a.
```
e = 3;
f = 2;
while (e >= 0)  {
        printf("%d %d\n", e, f);
        e = e - f;
        f = f - e;
}
printf("%d %d\n", e+4, f-3);
printf("%d %d\n", e, f);
```

b.
```
c = 3;
d = 4;
g = 20;
do  {
        if (c * d  < g)
                g += 100;
        else if (c % 2 == 0)
```

```
                    d += 2;
          else
                    d += 5;
          printf("%d %d %d\n", c, d, g);
                    c += 6;
     } while (c <= 12);
     printf("%d %d %d\n", c, d, g);
```

5.   Assume that you run the program shown below, with the aim of typing in each of the
         following lines of data, one line at a time.

```
          1 -7  5
          1  2  3
          5  5  5
          1  2  0
          5  2  0
         -8  5  2
          1  1  1
          5  2  1
```

(a) However, the way the program is written, it will stop before you have a chance to type
in all the data. What is the last line that you will be able to enter before the program ends?

(b) What will the program output before it stops?

```
#include <stdio.h>

void main()
{
     int a, b, c;

     printf("enter 3 integers");
     scanf("%d", &a);
     scanf("%d", &b);
     scanf("%d", &c);

     while (a < b || c != 0) {
          printf("%d %d %d ", a, b, c);

          if ( a == c && !(b < -2) )
                printf("good\n");
          else if (c == 5 || c > 12)
                printf("bad\n");
          else
```

```
                              printf("indifferent\n");

                    printf("enter 3 integers");
                    scanf("%d", &a);
                    scanf("%d", &b);
                    scanf("%d", &c);
              }
        }
```

(12 pts)
6.   Write a complete main program and function to do the following.

The main program will read an integer into a variable called **grade**. Then the main program should send **grade** to a function called **curvedletgrade**, and the main program should store the answer returned by the function in a variable called **letter** (a single character). The main program should then print both **grade** and **letter**.

The function **curvedletgrade** receives a single parameter: a numerical grade (an integer) called **mark**. When the function is called, **mark** will have a value from 0 to 100. The function returns a single character, depending upon the value of mark. If mark is 85 or above, the function will return 'A'. If mark is at least 70 but less than 85, the function will return 'B'. If mark is between 60 and 69, the function will return 'C'. Otherwise, the function will return 'D'.

(6 pts)
7.   Consider the following structure declaration:

```
        struct book {
              double code;
              char authorname[15];
              int subject[3];
              int pages;
        } library[100];
```

(a) Write a statement to print the code and the author's name for book number 34 in the library.

(b) Print all three subjects for books 6 and 7.

(c) Suppose we want to know how many books in the library have at least 250 pages. Write the statements necessary to print this. If there are no books with at least 250 pages, the program should say NONE.

Part II Conversions and Multiple Choice (12 points)

A.   Conversions: change each of the following into the requested equivalent:

1.   56 base 10   to   base 2   _____

2.   111011 base 2   to   base 16   _____

3.   F8 base 16   to   base 2   _____

4.   3E base 16   to   base 10   _____

5.   101101 base 2   to   base 10   _____

6. Two bytes are equivalent to _____ bits.

B.   Select the letter of the best answer.

1.   Which of the following statements about the compiler is correct?
        a. A compiler written in C is converted into machine language.
        b. A source program written in C is converted into machine language.
        c. An object program written in C is converted into Turbo.
        d. A source program written in machine language is converted into C.
        e. An object program written in machine language is converted into C.

                                                        1. ans. _____

2.   Which of the following hardware devices is NOT part of a typical microcomputer system?
        a. printer
        b. monitor
        c. drawing tablet
        d. connection to the network
        e. keyboard
                                                        2. ans. _____

3.   A compiler, a word processor, and a database management system are all examples of:
        a. microcode
        b. high-level languages
        c. low-level languages
        d. hardware
        e. software
                                                        3. ans. _____

4.   Approximately how many years ago did microcomputers first become commercially
        available:
        a. two years ago
        b. five to ten years ago
        c. fifteen to twenty years ago
        d. fifty years ago
        e. one hundred years ago

                                                                4. ans. _____

5.   Your own individual diskette (which holds your programs and data files), plays what role
        in the microcomputer system:
        a. main memory
        b. RAM (random access memory)
        c. ALU (arithmetic logical unit)
        d. auxiliary storage
        e. coprocessor chip

                                                                5. ans. _____

6.   Which of the following statements is NOT true?
        a. An operating system is a large set of programs.
        b. An operating system manages the orderly use of a computer system.
        c. An operating system is useful when you are using a microcomputer.
        d. An operating system is not needed when you are using a mainframe computer.
        e. An operating system used on IBM PC's or compatibles is called DOS.

                                                                6.ans. _____

Part III (25 pts)

Write a complete C program which will do the following:

(a)   Read a series of sentences, each with a maximum of 80 characters. Each sentence ends
        with a period. Print each sentence as it is read.

(b)   For each sentence read, call a function that will return an integer equal to the number of
        words in the sentence. (Assume that there is exactly one blank between words.) Print the
        number returned, together with an appropriate message.

(c)   Call a function that will change the following characters in the original sentence, as
        follows:

                    each A becomes V
                    each E becomes P
                    each I becomes $

each O becomes F
each U becomes B
each b̶ becomes J

Example: "HAVE A NICE WEEK." becomes "HVVPJVJN$CPJWPPK."

Print this coded sentence.

Repeat the process until the data values are exhausted, and then print "THE END" and
end the program.

PART III   ANSWERS TO SELECTED PROBLEMS

The answers to many of the problems are given below. Please note that there are many ways to organize a program to solve a given problem, and that the answer given here for any programming problem is not necessarily the only possible answer. Of course, the problems which require that you state what output will be printed usually have specific answers. Some of the problems have only partial answers given here.

The Turbo C compiler uses 80 columns for printing results. Since this book is only about 65 or 70 columns wide, the answers to the problems which ask what will be printed are often simulated— the column spacing is not exact. It is hoped that you will be able to recognize the output from this abbreviated format. In the discussion of string manipulations (Chapter 11), the output is indicated somewhat more exactly, with blank columns indicated by a **b** (a **b** with a line through it).

You should occasionally reread the directions in the front of the book on how to use these answers.

If you find any mistakes in this book, please bring them to the attention of your instructor.

CHAPTER 1 - BASIC PRINCIPLES

1.   Identifiers in Turbo C
      (1) must start with a letter (either upper or lower case) or underbar.
      (2) must contain only letters, digits, and/or underbar character.
      (3) must not be reserved words.
      (4) must not contain blanks, punctuation marks, or arithmetic operators.
      (5) may have a length up to 127 characters. (Some versions of C have much lower limits on the length of identifiers. ASCII C requires C compilers to distinguish variables based on the first 31 characters.

      C is case sensative, thus it is conventional to use only lowercase letters for user defined variables. **#define**d constants are usually written in all upper case. A user defined variable should not begin with the underbar as many system variables begin with the underbar.

2.   (a), (b), (c), (f), and (d) are not valid; they don't start with letters. All the others are valid.

3.   (a), (b), (d), (e), (f), and (g) are invalid. Any symbol other than a letter, underbar, or digit is not valid.

4.   (a), (b), and (c) are not valid because they contain blanks. (d) and (f) are not valid because they contain a minus sign (the hyphen). All the rest are valid.

5.   All of the answers are valid. However, not all versions of C would distinguish variables which are similar in their first 8 (non ASCII C) or first 31 (ASCII C) charactes but differ in characters beyond the 8th (or 31st) positions. Since C is case sensitive, choice (c) is not recommended as it can easily lead to hard to detect syntax errors.

6.   (b), (e), and (g) are all valid identifiers; the others are either reserved keywords or operators. However, (e) and (g) usually refer to the standard library input function and the predefined constant -1 respectively, and should not be redefined by the programmer.

7.   (e) is invalid because of the slash (/). (d) is most descriptive, but longer than (c), which is okay. (a) and (b) are poor pairs of names.

8.   (d) is short yet descriptive enough. (c) might lead to confusion, since the two names are so similar. All are valid in C.

9.   A keyword such as **while**, **for**, **int**, **if**, and **else** are words which have a special meaning in the C language and can not be used in any other context. **#define**d constants are assigned values by the programmer and/or in the standard libraries and can not be changed later on in the program.

10.   (a) starts with a digit; (b) blank appears in the variable; (c) contains a period; and (g) is a keyword; All are illegal. The rest are all valid identifiers.

11.   The **=** denotes *assignment*. The value on the right of this operator is evaluated, and the value is then placed into the memory position denoted at the left of the operator.

12.   (a) in C, multiplication is denoted by the asterisk (*). In algebra, a multiplication cross (×) may be used, or no sign may be used. (For example, ab means a times b in algebra. In C, **ab** might be the name of an identifier.)

        (b) The slash operator (/) in C represents real division if at least one of its operands is a real number (i.e., 5 / 2.0 = 2.5) and integer division if both of its operands are integers (i.e., 5 / 2 = 2).

13.   (a) has an expression to the left of an assignment operator. (e) has a radical sign. (f) has an illegal identifier (**2y**). The others are legal.

14.   In (a) and (f) the order makes no difference. In (g), there should not bee too much change. In each of tthe others the order is important.

15.   Since C automatically converts between types, all of the choices are legal. However, unexpected results may occur. For example, in (b) assigning a real number to an integer

variable would cause truncation to occur, so that the value of **number** would be 8, not 8.25.

16.   A space is not permitted bettween the # and the preprocessor directive include. The name of the included library *stdio.h* must be enclosed in angle brackets (<>) not braces ({}) which are used to indicate a compound statement. The fact that comments is spelled wrong makes no difference because it is inside the comment delimiters. **12y** is an invalid variable name as it begins with a number. **x + 2** is illegal on the left side of the assignment statement. **3x** is illegal as it must be written with an explicit multiplication sign (i.e., **3 * x**). The condition in the **if** statement must be surrounded by parenthesis. The printout of **y**, which has not been initialized, is a logical error. Finally, the phrase end main must be placed within comment delimeters. Here is a corrected version:

```
#include <stdio.h>
/* comants */
        void main()
{
        int x, y, y12;
        x = 5 -2;
        x = 3*x + 7;
        if (x > 10) printf("x is larger than 10");
        printf("\n%d", x);
} /* end main */
```

17.   (a) The division operator '/' when used with two integer operands represents integer division. Thus **half** is an integer and doubling any integer yields an even number; **odd_number** is odd because it is one more than an evan number.

    (b)
```
#include <stdio.h>
void main()
{
        int integer, half, even;
        scanf("%d", &integer);
        half = integer / 2;
        even = 2 * half;
        printf("%d\n", even);
}
```

    (c)
```
#include <stdio.h>
void main()
{
        int integer, one_third, divisible;
        scanf("%d", &integer);
        one_third = (integer + 2) / 3;
        divisible = 3 * one_third;
```

```
        printf("%d\n", divisible);
}
```

if **integer** is originally divisible by 3, no damage will be done. If **integer** is not divisible by 3, the added 2 will cause the next highest integer divisible by 3 to be calculated. Try three successive integers to test the segment.

18.   In C, arithmetic operations on integer numbers produce integer answers; on real numbers or a mixture of real and integer numbers, they produce real results.

```
1 1.000000
5 5.000000
25
25.000000
25.000000
5.000000
5
125
125.000000
```

19.
```
2
7.000000
1
9.800000
16.799999
```

20.
```
#include <stdio.h>
void main()
{
        int num, first, second, third;

        printf("Enter a three-digit number ");
        scanf("%d", &num);
        third = num % 10;
        num = num / 10;
        second = num % 10;
        first = num / 10;
        num = 100 * third + 10 * second + first;
        printf("%d\n", num);
}
```

21.
```
#include <stdio.h>
void main()
{
```

```
                int num, mid;

                printf("Enter zip code ");
                scanf("&num");
                num = num / 100;
                mid = num % 10;
                printf("%d\n", mid);
        }
```

22.   Precedence is first given to parentheses, which thus may be used by the programmer to change the order in which operations would otherwise occur. Then,
(1) The highest precedence is unary minus (for example, **x = -7;** or **x = -y;**)
(2) The multiplication, division and modulus (%) operators have next highest precedence, followed by the addition and subtraction operators. Thus if there is a multiplication and an addition operation in an assignment statement, the multiplication is done first.
(3) For operators having the same precedence, these operations are done from left to right.
As C has numerous operators, in addition to the simple arithmetic ones, it is recommended that the student refer to the complete operator precedence table found in your textbook.

23.   13
                8
                13

24.   (a)   17   (b)   6

25.   value_1 = 14   value_2 = 3   value_3 = 1
        (Note the order of operations.)

26.   (1)   (b) and (c)
        (2)   none
        (3)   (b) and (c) yield the same result.
                (d) and (e) yield the same result.

27.   (a)   y = *a * b - a * a) / (x * y * y * y);
        (b)   y = a * (1 + b) / (x + 1);
        (c)   y = (a + (1 + b) * (1 + b)) / (2 * a);
        (d)   y = (6 * a / b + 1) / (x - x * x);
        (e)   y = 6 * a - 2 * b;
        (f)   y = 2 * x * x * x;
        (g)   y = (2 * x) * (2 * x) * (2 * x);
        (h)   y = 2 * x * x * x;
        (i)   y = -(x * x);
        (j)   y = -x * (-x);
        (k)   y = -(x * x);
```
```

28.   y = (-b - sqrt(b * b - 4 * a * c)) / (2 * a);
       (**sqrt** is the function in the standard *math.h* library that gives you the square root of
       whatever is in the parentheses.)

29   3   90   2

30.   x = (a + 2 * b) / (c - 3 * d * d * d * d);
       x = (a + 2 * b * b) / (3 * c * d * d * d * d);

31.   1   30   64

32.   x = (2 * a + b) / (3 * c);
       x = 2 * a + b / (3 * c);

33.   7.000000

34.   (a)   y = (x + 1) / (x - 1);
       (b)   z = (x - 4 * x * y + y) / (x - 1);
       (c)   a = sqrt(r);
       (d)   x = (-b + sqrt(b * b - 4 * a * c)) / (2 * a);
       (e)   w = abs(x + y) / x;

35.   y = x * x + 7 * x - 1) / (x / 3 + 5);

36.   g = 11.000000
       h = -1.000000
       i = -4.000000
       j = 284.000000

37.   (a)   10.000000   (b)   13.000000

38.   (a)   s = (x - 3 * x * y + 1) / (x * y + (x + y) / (x - y));
       (b)   s = (b - 4 * a * c) / (2 * a);

39.   (a)   45.000000
       (b)   -6.000000
       (c)   37.000000

40.   (a)   a = 6   b = 7   c = 2
       (b)   x = 3.000000

41.   g = 8   h = 11   i = 18

42.   a = 3   b = 5   c = 5   x = 7   y = 1   z = 13

43.   2   3   15

44.   10   3   6   4   5   1

45.   i = 2   j = 2   k = 2   l = 3

46.   2   2   5   0   6   1

47.   The **E** in a real number (printed by the compputer or used by the programmer means "times ten to the power which follows." (Note that when you use the **E**, you do not use the multiplication operator.)

48.   100   -0.4   0.007
       0.25   -5   88888.8
       3   -0.6   -0.0009

49.   (a)   1   1   1
       (b)   200   200   200
       (c)   0.003   0.003   3000
       (d)   0.00004   0.00004   -400000
       (e)   -0.500   50.0   -50.0

50.   (a) Many different versions of these numbers may be used. One example is used for each.

                (i)   -1.0e-1   (v)   500e3
                (ii)   2E3   (vi)   6.02e23
                (iii)   3e-2   (vii)   7e11
                (iv)   4.0E-3

       (b)   (i)   -1.000000e-01   (v)   5.000000e+03
                (ii)   2.000000e+03   (vi)   6.020000e+23
                (iii)   3.000000e-02   (vii)   7.000000e+11
                (iv)   4.000000e-03

51.   (a)   -1.5000000e+03   (b)   7.02000000e-03   (c)   66660

52.   -0.00123   -80000
       1   0.123456
       100   0.000000016
       0.040   -80000
       2000   2.34

53.   One of many possible forms is given for each:

1e3	6.03e-3	-6E-2
1.23e0	1.0e-1	-6.78e2
6.04e1	-1.4E3	1.0e6
1e10	1.6e-4	6.02e23

54.   truncation
          0.500000

It is hazerdous to comapre real quantities, since there is truncation error in the last
decimal plces. In decimal arithmetic, there would be no truncation with these numbers.
However, the computer works with binary arithmetic, where 0.1 and 0.4 are repeating
fractions (like 1/3 expressed in decimal). The printout of the value is rounded, which
makes the situation even more confusing.

55.   no truncation
          0.500000

Binary arithmetic handles powers of 2 ($\frac{1}{4} = 2^{-2}$) exactly. However, it is still dangerous to
comapre real quantities for equality.

56.   The standard *math.h* library function **sqrt** returns the square root of the expression
      withhin its parentheses. The **abs** function retruns the absolute value of its arguments. **ceil**
      ceil finds the smallest integer not less than its arguments. Thus **ceil** changes a real
      number into an integer by rounding it up. **floor** finds the largest integer not greater than
      its arguments. Thus **floor** changes a real number to an integer by truncating the fractional
      part. **pow** raises its first argument to its second argument's power (i.e., **pow(x,y)** returns
      x^y.

57.   These standard *math.h* functions cannot be on the left side of an assignment statement.

58.   4   1   1.000000

59.   8.000000   1.414214
          2.500000   2.000000

60.   2   1.414214
          4   2.000000
          6   2.449490

61.   (a)   3.000000   (b)   0.000000
      (The square of a number must be 0 or positive. Therefore **min** will equal zero.)

62.   3   5   3

63.   10   10.500000

```
10    10.000000
13   .11.500000
13    12.000000
```

64.
```
10    10.500000
10    10.000000
13    11.500000
13    11.000000
```

65. It is not a legal statement, because although **sqrt()** is defined in the standard *math.h* library, declaring **sqrt** as a variable causes it to lose its meaning as a function.

66.
```
#include <stdio.h>
#include <math.h>
void main()
{
        float weight;
        int integer;

        scanf("%f", &weight);
        integer = floor(weight);
        printf("%d pounds and ", integer);
        weight = weight - integer;
        integer = floor(weight * 16);
        printf("%d ounces\n", integer);
}
```

67.
```
#include <stdio.h>
#include <math.h>
void main()
{
        float dollars, realwt;
        int cents, intwt;

        scanf("%f", &realwt);
        /* round weight up to next ounce */
        intwt = floor(realwt + 0.99);
        /* 5 cents extra for first ounce */
        cents = 5 + intwt * 17;
        dollars = cents / 100.0;   /* dividing by a real number */
                                   /* yields a real number      */
        printf("%5.2f", dollars);  /* numbers regulate format */
}
```

32,767 in Turbo C. If an integer answer exceed this value, an overflow occurs, and an incorrect (and possibly negative) answer results. If the intermediate answers are real, no such overflow occurs.

(a)   -6072
        0
        125000.000000
        -6072
        125000.000000

(b)   -6072   -6072

(c)   0
        125000.000000

CHAPTER 2 - CONDITIONAL BRANCHING

1. 7

2. (a) **if** (v < 0)
         q = sqrt(10);

   (b) **if** (count % 10 == 0)
          h = 3;

   (c) **if** (q != 0)
          z = floor(4.67 + 0.5);

   (d) **if** (x >= 0)
           i = 7;
      else
           i = 8;

3.
data	(a)	(b)	(c)
2 3	A LOWER	A NOT HIGHER	NOT EQUAL
3 3	A NOT LOWER	A NOT HIGHER	EQUAL
4 3	A NOT LOWER	A HIGHER	NOT EQUAL

4. Just because **a** is not lower than **B** does not mean that it is higher; it may be equal.

5. There is no use asking a question if the following statements do not depend on the answer. No matter what the relationship between **a** and **b**, **c** will be set equal to 12. Thus the statement **c = 12;** could be used in place of the statement given. While most students would not write such a statement, many do write statements such as

```
if (a > c) {
        z = 12;
        printf("%d", a);
}
else
        printf("%d", a);
```

which could be simplified to

```
if (a > c)
        z = 12;
printf("%d", a);
```

6.   b, c, d, f, h, i, k

7.
```
#include <stdio.h>
#include <math.h>
/* Calculate the cost to send a parcel,   */
/* given the parameters in the problem. */
void main()
{
        float weight, cost;

        printf("Enter the weight ");
        scanf("%f", &weight);
        if (weight > floor(weight))
                        weight = floor(weight + 1);
        if (weight <= 14)
                        cost = 0.45 * weight;
        else
                        cost = 6.30 + (weight - 14) * 0.36;
        if (cost < 3)
                        cost = 3;
        printf("Cost = %7.2f\n", cost);
}
```

8.   (a)   ```
if (x > 0)
        a = 5;
else
        a = 10;
```

        (b)      ```
if (x > 0)
        a = 5;
else
        a = 10;
```

        (c)   ```
if (x > 5 && x < 10)
        a = a + 1;
else
        a = a - 1;
```

        (d)      ```
if (x > 0)
        a = 6;
else
        a = 0;
```

9.   (a)   printf("%d", a);

(b)
```
if (a > b)              /* the braces are unnecessary */
        if (c > d)
                e = 12;
```

or

```
if (a > b && c > d)
        e = 12;
```

(c)
```
if (a > b)
        if (c > d)
                e = 12;
        else
                e = 19;
```

or

```
if (a > b && c > d)
        e = 12;
else
        e = 19;
```

10. (a)
```
if (x > y )
        a = b;
c = d;
e = f;
```

The last two assignment statements are not related to the **if** clause.and should not be indented.

(b)
```
if (a == b)
        if (c == d)
                e = f;
        else
                e = f + 2;
```

The **else** was under the wrong **if**.

(c)
```
if (a == b)
        if (c == d)
                e = f;
        else
                ;
        else
                e = f + 2;
```

The **else** clauses were aligned under the wrong **then** clauses.

(d) No correction is needed.

11.   (a)   **if** (a > z)   (b)   **if** (a > z)
                  x++;   **if** (b > y)
            else   x = 2;
                  x = y + z;   **else**
                                                               x = 7;

12.   show

13.   (a)   red
             green

      (b)   #include <stdio.h>
             void main()
             {
                   int a, b, c;

                   a = 5;
                   b = 6;
                   c = 7;
                   if (a == b)
                         if (c == b + 1)
                               printf("green\n");
                         else
                               printf("blue\n");
                   else
                         printf("red\n");

                   if (a == b - 1)
                         if (c == b + 1)
                               printf("green\n");
                         else
                               printf("blue\n");
                   else
                         printf("red\n");
             }

14.   (a)   **if** (a > b)
                   if (c > d)
                         e = e + 3;

```
                else
                        ;
        else
                e = e + 10;
        printf("e = %d", e);
```

(b)   **if** (a > b)
```
                if (c > d)
                        e = e + 3;
                else
                        e = e + 10;
        printf("e = %d", e);
```

(c)   **if** (a > b)
```
                if (c > d)
                        e = e + 3;
                else
                        e = e + 10;
        printf("e = %d", e);
```

output: (a) e = 1   (b) e = 11   (c) e = 11

15.   (a)   **if** (a >= 5)
```
                x = 66;
```

The one relational operator >= takes care of both conditions.

(b)   x = 99;
        y = 6;

Since **x** was just set to 99, it must be greater than 33.

16.   (a)   **if** (a >= b)
```
                x = -5;
        else
                x = 7;
```

(b)   a = b;

(c)   a = b;

17.   (a)   **if** (a == b)   (b)   **if** (! (a == b))
```
                x = -5;                          x = 5;
        else                            else
                x = 5;                           x = -5;
```

18.   `invalid`
         `19`

19.   (a) is equivalent to the first statement since **&&** has higher precedence than **||** or does.

20.   3   8   1

21.   e = 11
         e = 4
         e = 11
         e = 11
         e = 11
         e = 11
         e = 4
         e = 11

22.   (a)   **if** (x == y)
                 x--;
             else
                 x++;

      (b)   **if** (grade < 0 || grade > 100)
                 printf("GRADE INVALID");
             else
                 total = total + grade;

             or

             if (grade >= 0 && grade <= 100)
                 total = total + grade;
             else
                 printf("GRADE INVALID");

      (c)   **if** (a == b)
                 c = d;

      (d)   **if** (a >= b || (c >= d && c >= e))
                 x = 2;
             else
                 x = 1;

             or

             if (a < b && (c < d || c < e))

```
                    x = 1;
            else
                    x = 2;
```

23.   e = e + 3;   /* in any case */
                if (a <= b && c <= d)   /* 7 more   */
                    e = e + 7;

24.   (a) Any grade must be either <= 100 or >= 0. The || should be an **&&**.

        (b) No grade can be both < 0 and > 100. The **&&** should be an ||.

25.   (a)   **if** (a > b || c < d || e == f)
                    x = 1;

        (b)   **if** (a == b && c > d && e > f)
                    printf("%d", x);

        (c)   y = x;
                if (a > b)
                    w = x - 1;
                else
                    w = x + 1;

26.   **15   20   15**

27.   6   4   9   9

28.   (a) C evaluates conditional expressions using the technique of *short circuit evaluation*. That is, only enough of the expression is evaluated in order for a decision to be made. Thus in Part (i) the expression **x != 0** is evaluated first, while in Part (ii) the expression **y/x == 0** is evaluated first.

        (b) If **x** has the value of zero, Part (i) would evaluate properly (i.e. since an **&&** is false if *any* one of it clauses is *false*, as soon as the clause **x != 0** is found to be *false* the entire condition is known to be *false* and thus the devision by zero in the second clause is never evaluated. On the other hand, in Part (ii) since **y/x == 100** appearrs on the right hand side of the **&&**, it will be evaluated first. Thus in the case where **x** is zero, a logical error will occur.

29.   (a) The entire condition would need to be evaluated, since the computer cannot determine whether the || is *false* after only evaluating its first clause.

        (b) Only the first clause is evaluated since upon determining that it is *false*, no further evaluation need be done.

(c) Only the first clase is evaluated since immediately upon determining that the first clause is *true*, the entire expression is known to be true.

(d) Since **&&** has greater precedence than **||**, its value must be determined first. Once the clause **y == c** is determined to be *false*, there is no reason to evaluate **x != 0**. However, **x != y** still needs to be evaluated since if it turns out to be *true* (which in this case it is) the entire condition would still be *true*.

(e) Only the first clause, **x != y**, and the last clause, **x != 0** is evaluated. Due to the precedence rules this expression is evaluated as if it was written

$$(x\ !=\ y\ \&\&\ y\ ==\ c)\ ||\ x\ !=\ 0$$

The entire parentheses can be determined to be *false* as soon as its first clause is evaluated, and thus there is no need to evaluate the clause **y == c**. However, the last clause must be evaluated in order to determine the ultimate result, namely that the condition is *false*.

30. (a) 1
 (b)   0
 (c) Any *non*-zero value in C is considered to be logically *true*. Zero is interpreted as having the logical value of *false*.

31.

	value	logical interpretation	
(a)	0	*false*	
(b)	0	*false*	an assignment statement takes on the value assigned to its left hand side (known as an *lvalue*).
(c)	1	*true*	
(d)	15	*true*	
(e)	-5	*true*	see above. All non-zero values are considered to be logically *true*.
(f)	0	*false*	
(g)	-25	*true*	
(h)	1	*true*	the right hand side of the assignment statement is evaluated and is found to be *true*. The value 1 is then assigned to the valiable **c** which becomes the value of the entire statement.
(i)	-1	*true*	
(j)	0	*false*	

32. (a)   if (switch)

...

(**switch** is either zero or non-zero. If it is zero, then its logical interpretation is *false* and hence the condition is false. Thus *logically*, the condition has the same value as the variable itself, and the variable may be used alone.)

(b)   if (!switch)

...

(c)   if (sw1 && !sw2)

...

33.   **a == b** is a boolean expression, which is either *true* or *false*. Thus if **a** does equal **b**, the expression is *true* and a value of 1 is assigned to **flag**. Otherwise, **flag** is assigned the value 0.

34.   2   2   2   1

35.   0
        1
        1
        0
        true
        nonsense

36.   true
        false
        true

37.   (a)

a	b	c	!b	a && !b	a && !b || c
T	T	T	F	F	T
T	T	F	F	F	F
T	F	T	T	T	T
T	F	F	T	T	T
F	T	T	F	F	T
F	T	F	F	F	F
F	F	T	T	F	T
F	F	F	T	F	F

(b)

a	b	c	a && b	!(a && b)	!(a && b) || c
T	T	T	T	F	T
T	T	F	T	F	F
T	F	T	F	T	T
T	F	F	F	T	T
F	T	T	F	T	T
F	T	F	F	T	T
F	F	T	F	T	T
F	F	F	F	T	T

(c)

a	b	c	a || b	a && c	!(a && c)	(a || b) && !(a && c)
T	T	T	T	T	F	F
T	T	F	T	F	T	T
T	F	T	T	T	F	F
T	F	F	T	F	T	T
F	T	T	T	F	T	T
F	T	F	T	F	T	T
F	F	T	F	F	T	F
F	F	F	F	F	T	F

CHAPTER 3 - FLOWCHARTS

1.   (a)
```
if (a >= b)
        x = 4;
y = 6;
```
   (b)
```
if (a >= b)
            q = 11;
r = 13;
```

   (c)
```
if (a > b)
        x = 7;
else
        y = 8;
z = 9;
```

2.   (a)
```
if (c < d) {
        n = m + 1;
        z = 2;
}
else
        m = m + 1;
b = a + 2;
```
   (b)
```
if (p == q) {
        p = t;
        q = r;
}
else {
        q = t;
        p = r;
}
printf("%d", p);
```

   (c)
```
if (x > y)
        a = 1;
else {
        b = 2;
        a = 3;
}
c = 1;
```

3.   Part (a) has a null *true* clause, which could be made into a null **else** or better yet into no **else** at all. The code could be

```
if (a <= 7) {
        b++;
        c = b + 2;
}
```

Note that the greater than sign is changed to less than or equal, not merely less than.

Part (b) sets **x** to 7 no matter what the first condition turns out to be. Later it sets **z** equal to **x** whether it had been set equal to **y** previously or not. The flowchart and code could be simplified to

```
x = 7;
z = 7;
```

(c) Although it appears that **y** is set to the value of **x** whether or not **z** is zero, it makes a difference as to when it is set euwal to **x**. In either case, however, **x** is set equal to 5. The code is thus

```
if (z == 0)
        y = 5;
else
        y = x;
x = 5;
z = 5;
```

(d)
```
if (a == b)
        q = 7;
r = 8;
t = 10;
```

(e)
```
if (a > b)
        x = 7;
z = 9;              /* It is useless to set z equal to 8  when it will */
                    /* be immediately changed to 9 anyway.       */
```

(f)
```
y = 1;              /* The initial assignments can be ignored.    */
```

4.   (a)
```
if (a < 0)
        if (b == 7)
                c = 10;
                d = 11;
        else
                e = f - 5;
g = c - d;
```

(b)
```
if (a > b)
        if (c > d)
                e = f;
        else
                e = g;
else    if (h < r)
                r = r + 1;
        else
                r = h * r;
z = 9;
```

5.
```
scanf("%d", &a);
if (a > a * a)
        x = a - a * a;
else
        x = a * a - a;
printf("%d", x);
```

```
scanf("%d", &a);
x = abs(a - a * a);
printf("%d", x);
/* if a > a * a, then x is positive */
/* if a * a > a, x is still positive   */
```

6.
```
if (a > 10) {
        z = 2;
        if (c > f)
                b = c + 1;
        else
                d = c - 1;
}
else
        d = e - 1;
i = 17;
```

7. (a) There is no use in incrementing **x** twice.

```
if (x < 0)
        x = x + 4;
else
        x = x + 5;
```

   (b)
```
if (a > b)
        x = x + r + 6;
else
        x = x + r;
r = r + 6;
w = 7;
```

   (c)
```
if (a < b)
        x = 6 + x;
else
        x = r + x;
r = 6;
w = 17;
```

8.
```
sum = 0;
scanf("%d%d", &a, &b);
printf("%d   %d\n", a, b);
while (a > b) {
        sum = sum + a;
```

```
            a++;
        }
        printf("%d\n", sum);
```

9.   (a)   **if** (a > b)   **if** (a > b && c < d)
                  if (c < d)   z = 22;
                      z = 22;   q = i + a;
              q = i + a;

      (b)   **if** (a < b)   **if** (a < b || c > d)
                  z = 12;   z = 12;
              else   **if** (c > d)   q = z + 2;
                      z = 12;
              q = z + 2;

10.   scanf("%d%d%d", &a, &b, &c);
             if (h > 2 * b)
                  if (b > c)
                      b++;
                  else
                      ;
             else   **if** (a > b)
                      ;
                  else
                      a++;
             c++;

11.   (a)   **if** (a < 0)
                  if (b == 7)
                      c = 10;
                  else
                      ;
              else
                  e = f - 5;
             g = c - d;

      (b)   **if** (a < 0)
                  if (b == 7)
                      c = 10;
                  else
                      d = 11;
             g = c -d;
```

(c)  A null **else** is required in Part (a), but not in Part (b). It could be used in Part (b), but a *true* clause with a null **else** is the same as just a *true* clause if no other **else** clause
```

follows.

12.   (a)

```
if (a > 10) {
        z = 2;
        if (c > f)
                b = c + 1;
        else
                d = c - 1;
}
i = 17;
```

    (b)

```
if (a > 10) {
        z = 2;
        if (c > f)
                b = c + 1;
}
else
        d = e - 1;
i = 17;
```

(c) A null **else** is not required in either case. In Part (a), the one **else** clause completes the last **if**, and no further **else** clause is needed. In Part (b), the closing brace completes the first *true* clause, ensuring that the **else** which is present completes the first **if**.

13.

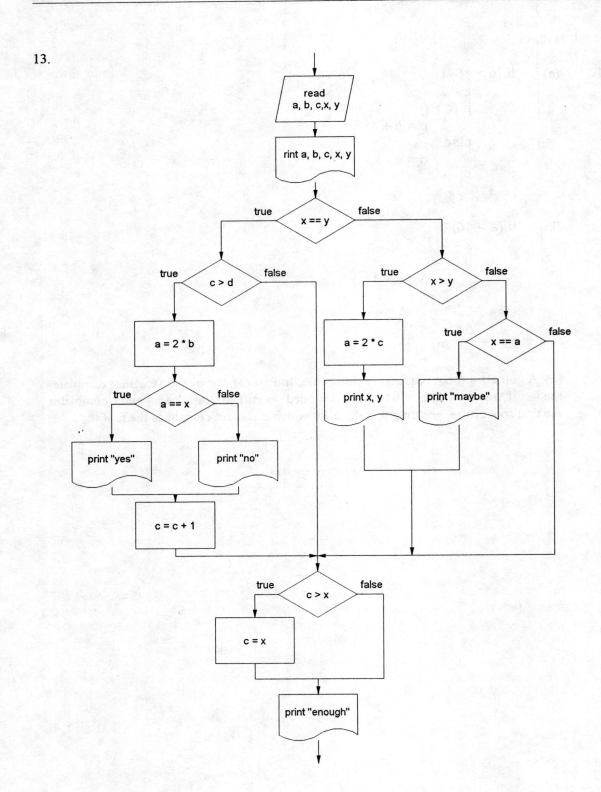

CHAPTER 4 - LOOP STRUCTURES

1.
```
x = 4     y = 2
x = 4     y = 3
x = 5     y = 4
the sum of x and y is 9
```

2.   (a)   4   (b)   2   (The loop in Part (b) keeps executing until **x = 2**.)

3.
```
B WINNER
A WINNER
B WINNER
3
```

4.   The **while** loop would not terminate as the condition would not be satisfied. Thus the body of the loop would be executed once again and the computer would pause for additional input to satisfy the **scanf** statement.

5.   (a)
```
1st is larger
1st is larger
1st is larger
1st is larger
1st is not larger
5 pairs were processed
```

(b)   A control-z (^Z), known as the *end-of-file*, signals the end of data whether typed in by the user or found at the end of an external data file. As soon as the **scanf** function detects the *end-of-file* it returns a -1 which immediately terminates the loop.

6.   The **scanf** function returns the number of items it successfully read or a -1 when it detects the *end-of-file*. Thus in the program of Question 5, an odd number of data items followed by a ^Z would terminate the loop and the program. In any event, the program would print the total number of *pairs* of data it had read.

7.   (a) In its simplest form, the **for** loop will execute the body of the loop the predetermined number of times, with no possibility of changing the number by calculations within the loop. It is usually used when the programmer knows ahead of time the number of times we wish to repeat the loop. (b) A **while** loop will execute as long as its condition remains *true*. It requires that any initializations be done prior to executing the loop. It is usually used when we don't know ahead of time the number of loops we wish to repeat the loop. However, an advanced form of the **for** loop is essentially interchangeable with the **while** loop.

8.   (a) An infinite number of 1's. (There is no change in the value of **i** within the loop.
      (b) 6 (The **printf** statement is not within the loop.)

9.   We must add the initialization and incrementation statements for **i**, and change the loop
      header.

```
i = 1;
count = 0;
sum = 0;
while (i <= 4) {
        sum = sum + i;
        count++;
        i++;
}
```

10.   The **scanf("%d", &b);** and the **scanf("%d %d", &b, &a);** statements.

11.   We intended to increment **x** by 1/3 each time through the loop. However, **x** will get to a
      value of 4.999999, but it will never be exactly 5. Changing != 5 to < 5 would stop the
      looping after four iterations.

12.   Look closely at the condition in the **while** loop. The programmer inadvertently used an
      assignment statement (**x = 0**) rather than a test for equality (**x == 0**). An assignment
      statement takes on the value assigned to the left hand side (known as the *lvalue*). Thus the
      expression in the **while** loop has the value of 0 which in C has the logical value of *false*.
      The condition is initially false and the body of the loop is never performed. This is a very
      common and difficult to find error.

13.   (a)   4   (b)   14   (c)   4   64   (d)   1   3
             2   20
             1
             1

14.   (a)   -1   (b)   0

15.   (a)   count = count - 1;
      (b)   Use **count**.
      (c)   count = count - 2;

16.   5
             10
             15
             10   4   15
             (*blank line*)
             -2   4   15

17.
```
10   4   10
 6   1   1
 6   3   6
-1000   1   1
```

18.
```
GOOD   4
GOOD   4
GOOD   4
ZZZ   3
ZZZZZZ
```

Leading and trailing blanks are ignored by the **%s** in the **scanf** statement. Therefore, the next to last line of data will terminate the **while** loop and the last line of data will not be processed.

19.   When the trailer value is reached, the execution continued (in the body of the loop) at the statement after the **scanf**, which caused the printing of the phony values and the extra count. On way to solve the problem is to put a **scanf** before the loop, and to move the **scanf** in the loop to the last statement in the loop. Then, when the trailer value is read, the next statement will send control back to the header, which will test and skip the loop. This is exactly what is desired.

20.   Compared with the program as corrected in the answer to Exercise 19, the version given here is more compact and elegant. The condition in the **while** header is known as a C *idiom*, that is an expression which is often used and with which the programmer should be comfortable. However, non-programmers using the program, may be unfamiliar with the use of the control-z (^Z) as an end-of-data sentinel and may be more comfortable with the use of a phony data item to flag the end-of-data.

21.
```
4   6   -2
-2
5   6   -1
-1
6   0
0
7   6   1
```

22.
```
2   8   0
2   8   0
```

23.   The **if** statement in the loop is meaningless; it must be true or the body of the loop would never have been entered in the first place. Thus the **else** clause can be eliminated, as well as the **if** statement. All that is left is

while (x <= 3 && y < 0) {

```
                        x = x - 1;
                        y = 2 * x + 4;
                        printf("%d  %d  %d\n", x, y, z);
                }
```

24.   The count of the number of grades is one too high. The average can be calculated
        correctly by initializing **count** to zero. In addition, the average is never printed out. This
        may be corrected by adding the statement

                printf("Average is %5.1f\n", ave);

        at the end of the program.

25.   8   16

26.   The table of numbers, square roots, and squares will have a "heading" every other line.
        The **printf("number ...** statement should precede the entire loop.

27.
```c
#include <stdio.h>
#include <string.h>
void main()
{
        char first[10], last[10];
        int smithcount = 0, johncount = 0, bothcount = 0;

        while (scanf("%s%s", last, first) == 2) {
                printf("%s, %s\n", last, first);
                if (strcmp(last, "SMITH") == 0)
                        smithcount++;
                if (strcmp(first, "JOHN") == 0)
                        johncount++;
                if (strcmp(last, "SMITH") == 0 && strcmp(first, "JOHN") == 0)
                        bothcount++;
        }
        printf("JOHN occurred %d times\n", johncount);
        printf("SMITH occurred %d times\n", smithcount);
        printf("JOHN SMITH occurred %d times\n", bothcount);
}
```

28.   4   7   7   3
                1   7   7   3
                11   4   13   7
                11   4   13   7

29.   An infinite number of 1's will be printed because the condition of the loop is always true.

30.   average 84
               EXCELLENT   GOOD   POOR

The -1 value serves as a trailer, to signal the end of one type of input (and the beginning of another type).

31.   **(a)**   305   8

       (b)   260.000000   7
                  37.142857

       (c)   305   8
                  38

32.   (a) No change. The statement sets **j** to the result of the comparison. Thus, if **a** is greater than 0, then the answer is *true*, and 1 is assigned to **j**. Otherwise, **j** is set to 0.

       (b) With the >= operator, the data values given will not cause the looping to end. A negative number is necessary to do that. If a negative number were added at the end of the data, the zero is counted as a real data point, and the results would be

              305   9
              33

       (c) The same answer as in Part (a). In this case, there are no negative values, so **a <> 0** will be false when **a > 0** is false.

33.   **(a)**   8
                  14
                  20

Testing two variables which have been declared to be of type **float** for equality is error prone because of the way real numbers are stored in memory.

       (b) Because **z** never equals 20, an infinite loop is created, with output starting

              9
              15
              21
              ...

34.   Small truncation errors might give **x** and **y** very slightly different values— what a human would consider tantamount to equal. However, the computer regards equal as exactly equal. The smallest differences would cause the loop to continue executing. In Part (b), a small difference between the variables will be recognized as a value nearly zero, and the looping will stop.

35.   (a)   7
        (b)   7   (subtract the first value from the last, and then add 1)

36.   (a)   10   4
        (b)   113   10   -1
        (c)   sum = 15   i = 6
        (d)   10   4

37.   (a)   10   4
        (b)   10   1
        (c)   4   4

The similar loops do very different calculations depending on the placement of the
initialization statements, as seen by these results.

38.   FINISHED

The loop is never executed since the limit is less than the initial value.

39.   (a)   3   9
                4   16
                5   25

        (b)   5   25

        (c)   3   9
                4   16

        (d)   0   0
                1   1
                2   4
                3   9
                4   16

        (e)   10   100
                9   81
                8   64
                7   49
                6   36
                5   25

        (f)   5

40.   B WINNER
                B WINNER

```
A WINNER
B WINNER
j = 3
```

41.   The semicolon makes the loop a null loop. The **j++;** statement is executed only once, after the loop ends.

42.   **e, f, g,** and **i** need not have been initialized. (Initialization of **d** is necessary whenever the **else** clause has not been executed before the **f = (c + d) / e;** statement, as in this case.

43.   (a)   7   4
              21   3
              42   2

       (b)   7   5
              28   5
              63   5

       (c)   7   5
              21   5
              42   5
              70   5
              105   5

Changing the value of the starting value (**n1**) within the loop does not effect the number of times the loop will be executed, since initialization only occurs once (before the loop is executed). However, changing any of the other variables in the second and third clause of the **for** statement will effect the number of times the loop will be performed, since these two clauses are re-evaluated each time the loop is performed. Changing the values of these variables is considered to be very poor style, and should be avoided.

44.   8   In C, a character is stored as an integer corresponding to its ASCII value. Thus the statement

       for (count = 'a'; count <= 'h'; count++)

is equivalent to the statement

       for (count = 65; count <= 72; count++)

45.   (a)   7   The two loops are independent of each other.

       (b)   12   These are *nested* loops for each time the outer loop (**for (i = 1; ...)** goes around once, the inner loop (**for (i = 1; ...)** goes around 4 times.

46.   (a)   20   5 ·   (b)   4   5

47.   **i**   **j**
       (a)   6   96
       (b)   10   160
       (c)   6   192

48.   7   32

49.   (a)   10   20
               11   22
               12   24
               13   26
               14   28
               15   30
               16   32
               17   34
               18   36
               19   38
               20   9

       (b)   In this case, the results are the same whichever way the condition is ordered. Since both clauses must be true for an **&&** to be true, both sides of the **&&** must be evaluated until one or the other is found to be false. **k < 20** becomes false before **m < 30** so **k < 20** is the clause which controls the loop.

50.   1   4
               2   5
               3   4
               4   1
               5   -4

51.   14   8

52.   1   5
               1   4
               1   3
               1   2
               1   1
               2   5
               2   4
               2   3
               2   2
               3   5
               3   4

```
3    3
4    5
4    4
5    5
```

53. The condition in a **while** loop is evaluated at the top of the loop prior to executing the body of the loop. The condition in a **do - while** loop is evaluated at the bottom of the loop after each execution of the body of the loop. Thus in the case where the condition is initially false, the body of a **while** loop will not be executed at all, while the body of a **do - while** loop will be executed one time.

54. The **while** loop usually requires an initialization before the loop, because the **while** condition normally checks the value of one or more variables. The **do - while** loop does not necessarily need to have an initialization before the loop, since the check on the condition is not done until the bottom of the loop. The initialization might be done within the loop.

55.
```
do {
        scanf("%d", &a);
        if (a != -1000) {
                sum = sum + a;
                i = i +1;
} while (a != 1000);
```

The **if** statement is necessary, since we must insure that the body is not performed when **a = -1000**.

56.
```
sum = 0;
scanf("%d%d", &a, &b);
printf("%d   %d\n", a, b);
do {
        sum = sum + a;
        a = a + 1;
} while (a <= b);
printf("%d\n", sum);
```

In Exercises 57 - 60, we may convert the **while** loop into a **do - while** loop directly, since we are sure that the body of the loop will be done at least one time (either because we are told so in Exercises 57-59 or because of the initialization of **i** which makes the condition initially true in Exercise 60. However, when converting the **while** loop into a **do - while** in Exercises 61 - 63, we must take into account the fact (explained in the answers to Exercises 53 and 54) that a **do - while** is always done at least one time, while a **while** loop, depending on the initial value of its condition, may not be executed even one time.

57.
```
do {
        /* body of loop */
} while (a > b);
```

58.
```
do {
        /* body of loop */
} while ( a > b && a == d);
```

59.
```
do {
        /* body of loop */
} while (a > b || a > d);
```

60.
```
i = 1;
do {
        scanf("%d", &i);
        /* body of loop */
} while (i <= 5);
```

61.
```
scanf("%d", &x);
do {
        if (x != 5) {
                /* body of loop */
                scanf("%d", &x);
        }
} while (x != 5);
```

We must repeat the **scanf** statement in the body of the **if** statement in order to insure that it is the value read from input that determines whether or not the loop is repeated and not any changes to **x** may have occurred within the /* *body of the loop* */. The programmer must be aware of these subtle differences when converting from one form to another.

62.
```
scanf("%d", &x);
/* body of loop */
scanf("%d", &x);
while (x !=5) {
        /* body of loop */
        scanf("%d", &x);
}
```

Note, that in the original **do - while** at least two input values for **x** will have been read before the condition in the **while** is evaluated. Our converted segment must reflect this as well.

63.
```
scanf("%d", &x);
do {
```

```
        if ( !abs(x) < 3) {
                /* body of loop */
                scanf("%d", &x);
        {
} while ( !abs(x) < 3);
```

64.   (a)   85   5   5
      (b)   98   10   -1
      (c)   30   3   15
      (d)   108   10   -1

65.   10   4   10
           6   1   1
           6   3   6

66.   (a)   4   5
      (b)   4   5
      (c)   4   5
      (d)   4   2

67.   (a)   Exceptional
           OK
           OK
           FAILING
           OK

(b) If the **break** statement were omitted, the computer would continue to "fall through" each subsequent **case** and print its message. The last **case** does not need a **break** since there are no other cases which follow.

68.   Mar   spring
          Err   error
          Jun   summer
          Nov   fall
          Sep   fall
          Apr   spring
          Dec   winter

69.   b a 98
          e b 101
          f x 102
          a b 97

          x 10

CHAPTER 5 - TURBO C INPUT/OUTPUT

1.   word is Hello

2.   123456
        123
        456

3.   (b) It is the control string that determines the format of the output. Since the **%s** formats are separated from each other, the words THE and END will print with several blanks between them.

4. | | statement | output |
        |---|---|---|
        | (a) | printf("%11.8f", x); | 13.6894005 |
        | (b) | printf("%7.5f", x); | 0.00321 |
        | (c) | printf("%6.4f", x); | 6.0562 |
        | (d) | printf("%12.8f", x); | −39.23046875 |
        | (e) | printf("%6.4f", x); | 0.0886 |

5.   (a) %e or %E

       (b) After the % of the format specifier but before the conversion character place an integer to specify the field width, followed by a decimal point and another integer to specify the precision (i.e. %width.precisionF). For example, **printf("%5.2d", x);** will print x in fixed form decimal form in a 5-column field with a decimal point and two decimal places, as 10.53.

       (c) If the field width is omitted, the computer will print the value to the specified precision in as much space as is needed to fit it in.

6.   The **#include <stdio.h>** preprocessor statement instructs the compiler to include at that point a "header file" which contains the definitions of the standard input/output functions such as **printf**, **scanf**, **getchar**, and many others.

7.   1 1

8.   12.3
         12.3
        12.30
        5.67
        5.7
          5.7

9.
```
          mickey   mouse      donaldduck
             mickey
               mouse
             donald
               duck
```

10.   (a) When we tabulate character information, we usually start in a given column. (see the telephone book, for example.) When we tabulate numeric information, we end in a given column (or we align decimal points). We would tabulate (by hand):

```
Adam, John              10.00
Burr, Aaron              1.98
Franklin, Benjamin      20.00
Washington, George     100.00
```

(b) To left justify a field, place a hyphen (-) prior to the field width. The default is right justification. Thus if **name** contained a string and **amount** represented a real number,

```
printf("%-20s%7.2\n", name, amount");
```

would print the results as tabulated above.

(c)
```
          Adam, John       10.00
         Burr, Aaron        1.98
  Franklin, Benjamin       20.00
  Washington, George      100.00
```

11.
```
    12345
    987612345
```

12.
```
    ohmygosh
    oh   my   gosh
    oh   my   gosh
```

13.
```
    quail   quaint   quake
    Will this be printed on a new line?   I think so.
```

14.
```
    12
    3.0000004.000000onetwo
    two12
```

15.
```
    16.0000000.31400
```

16.
```
    x = 1234.432861
```
            /* No field width or precision specified. **x** is printed in as   */

```
            /* many spaces as are required with a precision of 6, in    */
            /* fixed decimal format.                                     */
-x =  -1234.432861
            /* Same comment as above. The minus sign occupies a         */
            /* space.                                                    */
x =   1234.432861
            /* The field width of 8 is ignored as it is insufficient for x.  */
x =   1234.4329
            /* x is printed rounded to 4 decimal places, the field width of  */
            /* 9 is just enough.                                         */
x =   1234.433
            /* x is printed rounded to 3 decimal places, the field width of  */
            /* 8 is not enough so it is ignored.                         */
x =   1234.433
            /* x is printed rounded to 3 decimal places, the field width of  */
            /* 8 is just enough.                                         */
x =      1234.433
            /* x is printed rounded to 3 decimal places, right justified in  */
            /* a field width of 10.                                      */
```

17.   #define STRLEN 80
                  ...

             for (i = 1; i <= (STRLEN - strlen(word)) / 2; i++)
                     printf(" ");
             printf("%s\n", word);

For example, if the actual length of the string is 10, then the **for** loop will print (80-10)/2 or 35 blanks followed by the actual string. Thus there would be 35 blanks to the left and 35 blanks to the right of our 10 character string.

18.   (a)   scanf("%s%f", name, &num);

Note that the address operator (**&**) must be used when reading numbers and must *not* be used when reading strings. The statement will work successfully whether the data is entered on one line (separated by at least one blank) or whether the data is entered on separate lines.

         (b)   printf("%s\n%6.2f", name, num);

19.   34.000000
            5

The **5.6** is truncated when it is read into an **int** variable.

20. **number1 = 123, number2 = 456, number3 = 321.** In each case the **scanf** scans the
     input stream, *stdin*, until it has found a value for each of its parameters. It makes no
     difference whether the data is all on one line or spread out over more than one line. The
     extra data points are ignored (or will be read by subsequent **scanf** statements, if any).

21. *white space* is defined as any number of blanks, carriage returns, new lines, and/or tabs
     which come before or after a *non-white space* data item. The **%s** format specifier skips all
     white space which precedes a string and stops scanning upon encountering the white
     space which is after the string.

22. The standard library (*stdio.h*) function **scanf** scans the input stream, *stdin,* and after
     converting the data item into the format specified by the format specifier, places the value
     at the *location* at which the variable is stored. The address operator (**&**) returns the
     location or address of the variable to the **scanf** function. As you will learn in later
     chapters, a string variable is by definition a pointer to, or an address of, the string itself.
     Thus the address operator is not used since the variable is already an address.

23. In all four cases, **str = "delta"** and **num = 88.** As explained in the answer to Exercise
     21, the **%s** format specifier ignores all white space both before and after the string which
     is read.

24.
```
FILE * datafile;
datafile = fopen("test.dat", "r");
fscanf(datafile, "%d %d", &x, &y);
fclose(datafile);
```

25.
```
x = 1     y = 0      z = 1.000000
x = 2     y = 5      z = 1.414214
x = 3     y = 19     z = 1.732051
```

26. In all four cases, **str = "delta"** and **num = 88.** As explained in the answer to Exercise
     21, the **%s** format specifier ignores all white space both before and after the string which
     is read. **fscanf** is identical to **scanf**, except for the fact that the former reads from an
     external file while the latter will scan *stdin* (which is usually associated with the
     keyboard).

27. All three versions of the data file produce the same result:

```
begun
in loop
x = 1
in loop
x = 2
in loop
```

```
x = 3
in loop
x = 4
```

The conclusion is that the carriage returns at the end of the file do not effect the **scanf** function. The **scanf** function returns the number of items it has successfully read or a -1 (EOF) upon reaching the end of the file. This allows us to use the returned value within the condition of the **while** loop in order to signal when it is time to drop out of the loop.

28.   The first run produces

```
begun
in loop
x = 1
in loop
x = 2
in loop
x = 3
in loop
x = 4
```

The second and third runs produce the same output, with added output at the end. The extra carriage returns make the end of file appear later than the actual end of data. Thus the **feof** function returns *false* after having read the fourth integer and the loop is executed one additional time.

```
in loop
x = 4
```

The conclusion is that the **feof** function tests for the actual end of file, while the **scanf** function only tests whether or not there is any more data in the file (whether or not the file is actually at its end). Thus when using the **feof** function it is important not to put an extra carriage return at the end of the data file. It is for this reason that most C programmers use the C idiom of Exercise 27 when reading data from an external file.

29.   FILE * results;
       results = fopen("results.prt", "w");
       fclose(results);

30.   In order to direct the output to the printer, you would change the file referenced in the **fopen** function to point to the printers symbolic name.

       results = fopen("lpt1:", "w");

It is also a good idea to send a form feed to the printer, before the file is closed, so that any remaining output in the printer should be ejected.

```
fprintf(results, "\f");
fclose(results);
```

31.   The **w** file mode string instructs the computer to create a *new* file for your results. If a file with the same name already exists, it is *overwritten*. The **w+** file mode string also creates a new file for your results. However, if a file with the same name already exists, your output will be *appended* to the end of the existing file.

32.
```
#include <stdio.h>
void main()
{
        int test1, test2, test3;
        float average;
        char first[10], last[10];
        FILE * input, * output;

        input = fopen("input.dat", "r");
        output = fopen("output.dat", "w");

        while (fscanf(input, "%s%s%d%d%d",
                last, first, &test1, &test2, &test3) == 5) {

                average = (test1 + test2 + test3) / 3.0;
                fprintf(output, "%s %s    %3.0f", last, first, average);
        }

        fclose(input);
        fclose(output);
}
```

33.
```
#include <stdio.h>
#define MALE 0
#define FEMALE 1
void main()
{
        char first[10], last[10];
        int gender;
        FILE * names, * men, * women;

        names = fopen("names.dat", "r");
        men = fopen("men.out", "w");
        women = fopen("women.out", "w");
```

```
        while (fscanf(names, "%s%s%d", last, first, &gender) == 3 )
                if (gender == MALE)
                        fprintf(men, "%s %s\n", last, first);
                else
                        fprintf(women, "%s %s\n", last, first);

        fclose(names);
        fclose(men);
        fclose(women);
}
```

34. (a)   count = 1;
     (b)   count = 1;
     (c)   count = 0;

35. (a)   number_of_data = count + 1;
     (b)   number_of_data = count + 1;
     (c)   number_of_data = count;
     (d)   number_of_data = count;
     (e)   number_of_data = count - 1;

36. (a)
```
        10    4    10
         6    1     1
         6    3     6
```

     (b)
```
        10    4    10
         6    1     1
         6    3     6
       356    3     7
```

The program in Part (b) is flawed. It goes through the loop one extra time printing **a** despite it not having a current value. This occurs because the **fscanf** is at the top of the loop body and thus will not fall out of the loop upon encountering the end of file until it returns to the loop header. The proper method is used in Part (a), in which the **scanf** immediately precedes the condition in the **while** loop. Thus as soon as the **fscanf** runs out of data, the **while** loop condition is evaluated and the loop will be exited.

37. (a)
```
        GOOD     4
        GOOD     4
        GOOD     4
        MORNING      7
        MORNINGMORNING
```

     (b)
```
        GOOD     4
```

```
GOOD    4
GOOD    4
MORNINGMORNING
```

38. When the *end-of-file* was reached, the end of file condition was raised so that the body of the loop would not be repeated. But execution continued (in the body of the loop) at the statement after the **fscanf**, which caused the duplicate printing and extra count. One way to solve the problem is to put a **scanf** before the body of the loop, and to move the **fscanf** in the loop to the last statement in the body of the loop. Then, trying to read when there are no more values to be read will raise the *end-of-file* condition and the next statement will send control back to the header, which will test and skip the body of the loop, which is what is desired.

39. The program as written gives an incorrect answer for the average. This is due, as was explained in the previous answer, to repeating the loop one too many times and thus dividing the sum of the grades by one too many. It can be corrected by using the technique discussed in Exercise 38.

40.
```
305    8    45
```

41.
```
B WINNER
A WINNER
j = 2
```

CHAPTER 6 - INTEGER AND CHARACTER VARIABLES

1.   (a)   3   (b)   32   (c)   9

2,   a = 2   b = 4   c = 4
          x = 2.000000   y = 6.666667

3.   (a)   The largest integer that can be represented in two bytes is $2^{15} - 1 = 32{,}767$.
           The largest integer that can be represented in four bytes is $2^{31} - 1 =$
     2,147,483,647.

     (b)   On an IBM PC/compatible running Borland C++, an integer is stored in two bytes.
     Thus the largest integer is $2^{15} - 1$ (32,767). When using a typical workstation running
     Unix C, an integer is usually stored in four bytes, therefore the largest integer is $2^{31} - 1$
     (2,147,483,647).

4.   The value of the expression **a * 3** will exceed, *overflow*, the maximum value of an integer
     in Turbo C. This will yield an incorrect and possible negative value. It is the programmer's
     responsibility to make sure that no computation exceeds the limits for that variable or
     expression. In order to correct this the programmer could write

```
#include <stdio.h>
void main()
{
        int a;
        double b;

        a = 15000;
        b = a  * 3.0;
        printf("%d   %f\n", a, b);
}
```

     Note, that it is not enough to simply declare **b** as a **float** or **double**, we must also rewrite
     the assignment statement so that it involves a **double** expression (3.0).

5.   2   3   4   8   96

6.   1   1   1
          2   1   2
          3   1   3
          2   2   1
          4   4   4
          6   8   9

- 234 -

```
          3    3    1
          6    9    8
          9   27   27
```

7.
```
          1    0    0
          2    0    0
          3    0    0
          2    0    0
          4    0    0
          6    0    0
          3    0    0
          6    0    0
          9    0    0
```

Note the effect of using a mismatched conversion character which causes an **float** value to be incorrectly displayed as zero.

8.
```
          1    b    98
          2    c    99
          3    d    100
          4    e    101
          5    f    102
```

9.   According to the C language definition a variable whose type is **char** is stored in one byte. This is true regardless of which compiler or machine is used.

10.   If the integer is *unsigned*, such as an ASCII value, the largest integer that can be stored in one byte is $2^8 - 1 = 255$ (i.e., numbers in the range 0 .. 255). If the bits stored in one byte are to be treated as a *signed* number, the largest value would be $2^7 - 1 = 127$ (i.e., numbers in the range -127 .. +127).

11.   The program reads characters from *stdin*, one at a time until an *end-of-file* sentinel (i.e. control-z) is encountered and sends each character twice to *stdout*. If the keyboard and screen are used (i.e., the default *stdin* and *stdout*) the results would look as follows:

```
Hello<cr>
HHeelloo

Goodbye<cr>
GGooddbbyyee

<cr>
```

Note that all of the characters are duplicated even the carriage returns.

12.   EOF is defined in the standard library *stdio.h* as -1 and the ASCII value of the *end-of-file* sentinel is also -1. Recall from Exercise 9, that a **char** when treated as an ASCII value (i.e., an unsigned integer) can only contain the positive integers 0 .. 255. Because we need to be able to retrieve the *end-of-file* character using **getchar**, and then assign it to **c** so that it can be compared with EOF, it is necessary that **c** be declared to be of type **int.**

      As a general rule, anytime the C idiom **while ((c = getchar()) != EOF) { ...** is used, you should declare **c** as **int**.

13.   (a)   C> double   < a:infile.dat

            This is known as *input redirection*, which allows us to change the source of *stdin*.

      (b)   C> double   <a:infile.dat   > lpt1:

            In addition to *input redirection*, we are also indicating *output redirection*, which allows us to change the target of *stdout* from the default screen to, in this case, the printer (lpt1:).

14.   aaabbcc7   Only lowercase letters are printed and counted.

15.   The Cat In The   The output will be double spaced.

      Hat

      And

      The Cat in the Hat

      Comes Back

      1 Cat, 2 Cats, 3 Cats

16.   THE CAT IN THE   The output will be capitalized and the number of
      HAT   lowercase letters in the original data will be
      AND   counted.
      THE CAT IN THE HAT
      COMES BACK
      1 CAT, 2 CATS, 3 CATS
      37

17.   tHE cAT iN tHE   The program reverses the case of the input and
      hAT   counts the number of lowercase, uppercase, digits,
      aND   and total number of characters.
      tHE cAT IN THE hAT

```
          cOMES bACK
          1 cAT, 2 cATS, 3 cATS
          75       37      14      3
```

18.   Number: 90   85   110   51
          Characters: Z   U   n   3

Chapter 7 - Functions

1.
```
-14    1    -15
 6     2     8
 5     4     1
```

2.
```
y is bigger
x is bigger
y is bigger
```

3.
```
-14    1    second is bigger
 6     2    first is bigger
 5     4    second is bigger
```

4.
```
float cuberoot(float x)
{
        return pow(x, 1.0/3.0);
}
```

cuberoot isn't in the standard library because it might as well be done inline using the standard *math.h* library **pow** function directly.

5.
```
2    4    16
2    16   16
4    16   16
```

6.
```
#define TRUE 1
#define FALSE 0
#include <math.h>
int function(int x, int y)
{
        if (y <= sqrt(x) && y >= pow(x, 1.0/3.0))
                return TRUE;
        else
                return FALSE;

}
```

7.
```
float factorial(int n)
{
        int i;
        float product = 1.0;
```

```
            for (i = 1; i <= n; i++)
                    product = product * i;
            return product;
    }
```

8.
```
        float prodig(float a, float b, float c)
        {
                float largest, nextlargest;

                largest = a;
                nextlargest = b;
                if (b > largest) {
                        largest = b;
                        nextlargest = a;
                }
                if (c > largest){
                        nextlargest = largest;
                        largest = c;
                }
                else    if (c > nextlargest)
                        nextlargest = c;
                return largest * nextlargest;
        }
```

9.
```
        int biggest(int x, int y, int z)
        {
                if (x > y && x > z)
                        return x;
                else if (y > z)
                        return y;
                else
                        return z;
        }
```

10. (a) The same identifier cannot be used for the function and its parameter. If this is a function header then it must not end with a semicolon. If it is a function prototype the parameter identifier is not required (and is usually omitted).

(b) A function header must begin with a name of a type not a variable. Each parameter must be individually declared. For example,

```
        int func(int a, int b)
```

11.
```
        1   8   8
       -48  8   8
```

12.   (a)   *function header*:   **int** func(**int** b, **int** a)

       (b)   *function prototype*:   **int** func(**int**, **int**);
       (c)   *function invocation*:   c = func(a, b);   and
                                         a = func(b, a);

       (d)   *function definition*:   **int** func(**int** b, **int** a)
                                         {
                                                 int d;

                                                 d = a * b - b * b;
                                                 return d + b;
                                         }

13.   A *function prototype* allows the compiler to check whether or not the function is being
       invoked with the right number and type of parameters even if the function is not defined in
       the same file (or compiled at the same time) as the calling program.

       A *function header* does not end with a semicolon, while a *function prototype* does. Since
       the parameter names themselves are irrelevant to the syntax of the function, it is
       conventional when writing *function prototypes* to omit the parameter names. For example,
       compare the answers to Exercise 12 (a) and (b).

14.   (a) **double** is a keyword and may not be used as a variable.

       (b) **func** may not be used at the same time as an identifier for a function and a variable .

       (c) no error

15.   -2   4
           -2   4   2   4   8
           -2   4   10   -8   3

16.   5   4   2   answer: 10
           5   2   10   answer: 12

17.   4   3   1   3   5   20

18.   **int** addem(**int** n)
           {
                   int i, sum = 0;

                   for (i = 1; i <= ; i++)
                           sum = sum + i;

```
                    return sum;
        }

19.         int addem2(int n)
            {
                    int i,  sum = 0;

                    limit = abs(n);        /* abs returns the absolute value of n */
                    for (i = 1; i <= limit; i++)
                            sum = sum + i;
                    if (n > 0)
                            return sum;
                    else
                            return -sum;
        }
```

20.
```
        5    1    3     answer:    -2
        2    3   -2     answer:    36
```

21. The prototype for the function indicates that the parameter is expected to be of type **int [ ]**, which is an array (technically a pointer, i.e., **int ***), and returns a single value of type **int**.

(a) is invalid since the argument is a single array element (which is an **int**) rather than an entire array (**int ***).

(b) is invalid, since you may not return a single integer (which is of type **int**) and assign it to an array (which is of type **int ***).

22.
```
            char * agerange(int age)
            {
                    if (age <= 9)
                            return "child";
                    else if (age <= 19)
                            return "teens";
                    else if (age <=29)
                            return "twenties";
                    else if (age <= 39)
                            return "thirties";
                    else if (age <= 49)
                            return "forties";
                    else if (age <= 59)
                            return "fifties";
                    else if (age <= 69)
                            return "sixties";
```

```
            else if (age <= 79)
                    return "seventies";
            else if (age <= 89)
                    return "eighties";
            else    return "nineties";
    }
```

Assuming we had declared earlier in our program

```
    char message[20];
    char * agerange(int);
```

we could invoke the function by writing:

```
    strcpy(message, agerange(age));
```

or simply

```
    printf("%s", agerange(age));
```

23.
```
    void convert(float weight)
    {
            float pounds, ounces;

            pounds = floor(weight);
            ounces = floor((weight - pounds) * 16);
            printf("%5.0f pounds %2.0f ounces",pounds, ounces);
    }
```

24.
```
    two
    one
    three
```

25.
```
    float money(float principal,
                float rate,
                int deposit_year,
                int withdrawal_year)
    {
            int year;

            for (year = deposit_year; year <= withdrawal_year; year++)
                    principal = principal * (1 + rate);
            return principal;
    }
```

26.
```
void testmeans(float *pw, float *px, float *py, float *pz)
{
        float mean1, mean2;

        mean1 = (*pw + *px) / 2;
        mean2 = (*py + *pz) / 2;

        if (mean1 > mean2) {
                *pw = 8.6;
                *px = 8.6;
                *py = 8.6;
                *pz = 8.6;
        }
        else {
                *pw = 0.9;
                *px = 0.9;
                *py = 0.9;
                *pz = 0.9;
        }
}
```

27. In a *call by value*, the default method of passing parameters in C, the value of the argument is sent to the function and stored in a new memory location which has been labeled with the parameter's identifier. Any change made to the value of the parameter in the function is not reflected in its value in the calling program. It is for this reason that parameters that are passed by value are also known as *input parameters* since they serve to bring information into the function.

A *call by reference* (which is not directly supported by the C language), on the other hand, involves sending the address of the argument to a parameter which has been declared to be a pointer. No new storage is assigned to the parameter. Thus any reference to the memory location pointed to by the parameter refers to the original value which has been stored at that location. Any change of the value pointed to by the parameter within the function will modify the original argument. Parameters sent by reference are often known as *input/output parameters* since they serve to bring information into the function as well as sent information back to the calling program. When using a call by reference, the programmer must remember to refer to the parameter using the indirection operator (***p**), and to the send the address of the argument (**&x**) rather than the argument itself.

28.
```
#include <stdio.h>
#include <string.h>
void main()
{
        int test1, test2, final;
```

```c
        float average, highest = 0;
        char name[15], namehi[15];
        int readdata(char *, int *, int *, int *);
        float finalgrade(int, int, int);

        printf("%-20s%5s%10s%10s%10s\n",
                    "NAME","TEST1", "TEST2", "FINAL", "AVERAGE");
        while (readdata(name, &test1, &test2, &final) != EOF) {
                average = finalgrade(test1, test2, final);
                printf("%-20s%5d%10d%10d%10.1f\n",
                        name, test1, test2, final, average);
                if (average > highest) {
                        highest = average;
                        strcpy(namehi, name);
                }
        }
        printf("\n\n%s received the highest score which was %5.1f\n",
                namehi, highest);
}

/* Function readdata reads each line of data and returns EOF      */
/* there is no more data.                                         */
int readdata(char *name, int *ptest1, int *ptest2, int *pfinal)
{
        int errorfree(int);

        if (scanf("%s%d%d%d", name, ptest1, ptest2, pfinal) != 4)
                return EOF;
        *ptest1 = errorfree(*ptest1);
        *ptest2 = errorfree(*ptest2);
        *pfinal = errorfree(*pfinal);
        return !EOF;
}

/* Function errorfree checks a grade for validity and corrects it if   */
/* necessary.                                                          */
int errorfree(int grade)
{
        if (grade < 0)
                grade = -grade;
        while (grade > 100)
                grade = grade - 100;
        return grade;
}
```

```
/* Function finalgrade computes a final numeric average.          */
float finalgrade(int test1, int test2, int final)
{
        return 0.25 * test1 + 0.25 * test2 + 0.5 * final;
}
```

29.
```
3      -5      2
8      -5      -1
8       8      -9
```

30.
```
/* The result is x to the p power (if p is not negative) */
float raise(float x, float p)
{
        int c = 1;
        float result = 1;

        while (c <= p) {
                result  = result * x;
                c++;
        }
        return result;
}
```

31.
```
4      6      7
4      7      10
```

32.
```
void intquot(int x, int y, int *zp)
{
        if (x % y == 0)
                *pz = x / y;
        else
                *pz = x / y + 1;
}
```

33.
```
3      4      30      100
3      8      30      100
       50
```

34.
```
6      7      5
7      5      7
14      15      16
14      15      16
9      3      2
3      2      3
3      2      3
```

35.   4   10   3   20
             4   4   3   3

36.   An *input parameter* is a parameter which bring information *into* the function being called, but does not reflect any changes made to it back to the calling program. For example, **superb** in Exercise 33.

An *output parameter* is a parameter which has not been passed a value from the calling program, but receives a value from the function and reflects it back to the calling program. In order to do this it must be a pointer to a memory location established in the calling program (i.e., a *call by reference*). For example, **pz** in Exercise 29.

An *input/output parameter* brings information into the function being called and reflects any changes made to it back to the calling program. For example, **px** in Exercise 29.

A *local variable* is a variable declared within a function, which has no relationship with any variable (even if they share the same identifier) elsewhere in the program. For Example, **d** in Exercise 29.

37.
```
#include <math.h>
int func(int x, int y)
{
        int i;

        for( i = 1; i <= x, i++)
                if (pow(y, i) > x)
                        return i--;
}
```

38.
```
void func(int a, int b, char * c)
{
        if (b == 0)
                c = "Division by zero";
        else
                printf("%d", a / b);
}
```

39.   3
             4
             4
             5
             7

40.   2   3   4

```
5    5    6
5    7    9
-10   10    22
```

41.   TRUE
         1.000000
         0

42.   The function prototype does not match either the function header or the function invocation. Note that the third parameter is inconsistent, (1) **z** has been declared to be of type **int**; (2) the function header refers to an address, **float *c**, while the function prototype refers to a variable of type **float**; (3) if we assume that the function is written correctly, then the call to the function must use the address operator (**&**) for the third argument. The corrected program is as follows:

```
#include <stdio.h>
#define N 10
#define DOUBLE 2 * N
void main()
{
        int x, y, z;
        int fun(int, int, int *);

        x = N;
        y = DOUBLE;
        z = 66;
        x = fun(x, y, &z);
        printf("%d   %d   %d\n", x, y, z);
}

int fun(int a, int b, int *c)
{
        a = a + 1;
        b = b + 2;
        *c = *c + 3;
        return a + b + *c;
}
```

which when run produces the result:

```
102    20    69
```

43.   The function returns *true*, 1, if any element in the array has the same value as its subscript; otherwise it returns *false*, 0.

44.   (a)   ```
              float sumpart(float arr[], int lim1, int lim2)
              {
                      float sum = 0;
                      int i;

                      for (i = lim1; i <= lim2; i++)
                              sum = sum + arr[i];
                      return sum;
              }
              ```

       (b)    ```
              float partsum(float[][10], int rowx, int coly)
              {
                      int i, sum = 0;

                      for (i = 0; i < 10; i++)
                              sum = sum + arr[rowx][i];
                      for (i = 0; i < 5; i++)
                              sum = sum + arr[i][coly];
                      return sum;
              }
              ```

45.   12

46.    ```
       int func(int arr[], int n)
       {
               int i, smallest = 0;

               for (i = 0; i < n; i++)
                       if (arr[i] < smallest && arr[i] > 0)
                               smallest = arr[i];

               return sum;
       }
       ```

47.    ```
       float hiloavg(int arr[], int n)
       {
               int i, smallest, highest;

               smallest = highest = arr[0];
               for (i = 1; i < n; i++) {
                       if (smallest > arr[i])
                               smallest = arr[i];
                       if (highest < arr[i])
                               highest = arr[i];
       }
       ```

```
                                printf("smallest = %d   highest = %d\n", smallest, highest);
                                return (smallest + largest) / 2.0;
                        }

48.             void settoten(int arr[], int n, int *pk)
                {
                        int i;

                        *pk = 0;
                        for (i = 0; i < n; i++)
                                if (arr[i] > 10) {
                                        arr[i] = 10;
                                        *pk++;
                                }
                }

49.             void fixit(int arr[], int n)
                {
                        int i;

                        for (i = 0; i <= n; i++)
                                arr[i] = arr[i] * 2;
                        for (i = n+ 1; i < 50; i++)
                                arr[i] = arr[i] * 3;
                }

50.             void putpart(int arr[], int n)
                {
                        int i;

                        for (i = 0; i < 10; i++)
                                if (i < n)
                                        arr[i] = arr[i] + 5;
                                else
                                        arr[i] = arr[i] + 10;
                }

51.             void assign(int arr[][6], int n, int arr2[])
                {
                        int i;

                        for (i = 0; i < 6; i++)
                                arr2[i] = arr[n][i];
                }
```

52.   *function prototype*:

        void alpha(**char** [][30], **int**, **char** *, **char** *);

        void alpha(**char** person[][30], **int** n, **char** *first, **char** *last)

```
void alpha(char person[][30], int n, char *first, char *last)
{
        strcpy(first, person[0]);
        strcpy(last, person[n-1]) ;
}
```

53.   The variable **i** is a *global variable*, declared before any of the functions are defined. It is reset to 1 each time the function is called, and it never gets past 2. Thus the **while** loop in the main function is never ended. This type of error which is often very difficult to find is known as a *side effect* error, because it is caused as a side effect of executing the function. It can easily be avoided, and this program corrected, by declaring the variables within the body of the function in which they will be used. Variables declared within the body of a function are known as *local variables*; they are unrelated and therefore do not affect any other variable with the same name used elsewhere in the program. It is for this reason that the use of global variables is strongly discouraged.

54.   Use of **printtitle** in Part (b) requires 100 calls to the function, with the attendant overhead of the calls. Function **printall** in Part (a) prints the same titles with just one function call, and thus is much more efficient.

CHAPTER 8 - POINTERS AND REDIRECTION

1. The *address operator* (**&**) returns the address of its operand, while the *indirection operator* (*****) returns the value stored at the address pointed to by its operand. Both the address operator and the indirection operator are *unary* operators (i.e., they operate on a single operand like, for example, negation). The *bit-wise and* and the *multiplication* operators are both *binary* operators (i.e. they appear between two operands).

2.   5   5

3.   5   6
                6   5

4.   0   0   0   1   2

The first three answers above represent the subtraction of 8 - 8. **x** - **y** means the value of **x** minus the value of **y**. Similarly, ***p** - ***q** means the value stored at the address pointed to by **p** minus the value stored at the address pointed to by **q**. The same result is obtained when we write **x** - ***q** which is computed as the value of **x** minus the value stored at the address pointed to by **q**.

The last two answers may differ when run on different machines. **p** - **q** is computed using *pointer* arithmetic. When subtracting (or adding) pointers the computer returns an answer in *units* of storage. For example, since both **p** and **q** were declared to be pointers to an integer, and since an integer occupies two bytes in Turbo C, then if **x** was stored at address 0x302 and **y** at address 0x300, then **x** is one unit (an integer = 2 bytes) away from **y** and therefore **p** - **q** = 1. Using the *cast operator* on **p** and **q**, converts them from pointers into ordinary integers. Thus the result of **(int) p** - **(int) q** = 0x302 - 0x300 = 2.

5. All three loops are identical. The value of sum is 18.

6.   10   8   6   4   2   0   -2   -4   -6   -8
            10   99   6   4   2   99   -2   -4   -6   -8

7. (a) 3   (b) 3
    (c) 1   (d) 3
    (e) 3   (f) 0
    (g) 1   (h) 2
    (i) 1   (j) 2

8.   100   201   2   3   201   201   4

9.   0   1   2   77

```
        0    1    2
        1    2    1    2
```

10.   (a)   0   (b)   1
       (c)   2   (d)   77
       (e)   2   (f)   1
       (g)   2   (h)   1

CHAPTER 9 - ARRAYS

1.
```
6
5
3
2
9
```

2. Array **a** contains 10 elements; its upper bound is 9. Array **b** contains 15 elements; its upper bound is 14. All arrays in C have a lower bound of 0.

3.
10	20	30	40	50

4. (a) (i)   0
       (ii) 0

   (b) (i)   0
       (ii) 2
       (iii) 1
       (iv) 0

(In (b)(i), the answer is the product of **b[1]**, which is 0, and **b[9]**, which is 1.

5.

(a)	(b)		(c)		
10	0	0	0	0	0
20	1	2	1	1	1
30	2	4	2	2	2
40	3	6	3	3	3
50	4	8	4	4	4
	0	2			
	1	2			
	2	2			
	3	2			
	4	2			

6.

(a)	(b)	(c)	
1	8	0	1
2	8	1	1
3	8	2	1
4	8	3	1
5	8	4	1
6	8	5	1
7	8	6	1
8	8	7	1

	?		8		8	1
	?		8		9	0

(d) 0 0
    1 0
    2 0
    3 0
    4 0
    5 0
    6 0
    7 0
    8 0
    9 1

7. (a) **grades** and **stud_num** would be one possibility.
    (b) **num_of_students** and range are a possible pair.

8. Referring to an array element which is outside of the declared array is known as a *subscriptrange error* and is an example of an execution error. The C compiler will *not* issue any error or warning message and the results are unpredictable. Changing the contents of a memory location not contained within the storage allocated to the array may result in corruption of important data items necessary for the functioning of the computer and often leads to the machine freezing up— necessitating a complete reset of the computer.

9. (a) Array **a** contains the values 1 through 4, and array **b** contains the values 5 through 8.
    (b) Array **a** contains the values 1, 3, 5, and 7, while array **b** contains the values 2, 4, 6, and 8.

10. (a) 10 10 10 15 15 (After **a[2]** is changed to 10, this new value is added to the remaining elements.)

    (b) 10 10 10 10 10 (5, the original value of a[2], is added to each element.)

11.
```
int arr[10], x, i;
  ...
x = arr[3];
for (i = 0; i < 10; i++)
        arr[i] = arr[i] + x;
```

12.
```
int a[20], b[20], i;
  ...
for (i = 0; i < 10; i++)
        b[10 + i] = a[i];
```

13.
```
int a[100], b[10], i;
    ...
for (i = 0; i < 10; i++)
        b[i] = 2 * a[90 + i];
```

14. The first **for** loop takes **i** from 1 through 9. **a[0]** is never assigned a value and should not be printed in the second loop. Furthermore, on the last time through the first **for** loop when **i** is assigned the value 9, the statement **a[i+1] = a[i];** causes a *subscriptrange error* because the array **a** has only been assigned storage for elements **a[0]** through **a[9]**. An error message will not be generated, but the results of the program are unpredictable. The corrected program is as follows:

```
int a[10], i, j;
    ...
for (i = 0; i < 9; i++) {
        a[i] = i;
        printf("%d  ", a[i]);
        a[i] = a[i] + 1;
        a[i + 1] = a[i];
}
for (i = 0; i < 10; i++)
        printf("%d\n", a[i]);
```

15.
```
98   0   1
7    1   5
6    2   3
98   7   6   2   3   5   1
```

16.
```
#include <stdio.h>
#define MAXINT 32767
void main()
{
        int i, j, largest, a[50];
        float sum = 0, average;

        i = 0;
        while (scanf("%d", &a[i]) != EOF) {
                printf("%d  ", a[i]);
                sum = sum + a[i];
                i++;
        }
        average = sum / i;

        largest = -MAXINT;
```

```
                    for (j = 0; j < i; j++)
                            if (a[j] > largest && a[j] < average)
                                    largest = a[j];

                    printf("average = %f and largest less than average = %d.\n",
                            average, largest);
            }
```

An array is necessary for this program since all the data items need to be read in order to computer the average. Only after the average has been computed can we compare the average with all the data items which have been previously read.

17.   0
             0
             3
             9
             2

18.   3   9   2   4   7   0   18   12   9   1   3   9   2   4   7

19.   7 0 2 0 2 2 4 0 1 1 7 0 1 0 16 2 8 1 3 0
             0 2 2 1 1 0 0 2 1 0

20.
```
/* Missing portion goes here. */
large = small = number[0];
for (i = 1; i < n; i++) {
        if (number[i] > large)
                large = number[i];
        if (number[i] < small)
                small = number[i];
}
```

An array is not necessary for this task, since once an element has been compared with **large** and **small** it is not necessary to reexamine that element.

21.
```
for (i = n; i >= 1; i--)
        a[i] = a[i-1];
a[0] = 0;
```

22.
```
#include <stdio.h>
#define MAXITEMS 50
void main ()
{
        char names[MAXITEMS][10];
        int weight[MAXITEMS], i, count;
```

257

```
        float sum = 0.0, average;
        FILE * datafile;

        datafile = fopen("data.dat", "r");
        i = 0;
        while (fscanf(datafile, "%s%d", names[i], &weight[i]) == 2) {
                sum = sum + weight[i];
                i++;
        }
        count = i;
        average = sum / count;

        for (i = 0; i < count; i++)
                if (weight[i] > average - 20 && weight[i] < average + 20)
                        printf("%s\n", names[i]);

        fclose(datafile);
}
```

23.
```
        7
        21
        7
        7
        7
        7
```

24.
```
        -5    7    3    5    9
        0     7
        1     6
        2     15
        3     36
        4     17
```

25.
```
    yyyc
    y
    y
    y
    z
    b
```

26.
```
    3    spring
    6    summer
    9    fall
    12   winter
    0    error
```

```
        15   error
         2   winter
         5   spring
         8   summer
```

27.   98   7   6   2   3   5   1

28.   0   0   3   9   11   12   0   0   0   8

29.   One good set of identifiers would be **sales** for the array, and **dept** and **branch** for the subscripts.

30.   **a**: 20   **b**: 5   **c**: 24

31.   (a)   3   6   9   12   15   18   21   24   27   30   33   36
       (b)   12   24   36   9   21   33   6   18   30   3   15   27
       (c)   3   15   27   6   18   30   9   21   33   12   24   36

32.   8

33.   5   0   -2
       1   1   2
       -1   -1   1   -1   0   -1   0   -1   0   -1
       second
       -1   1   0   0   0   -1   -1   -1   -1   -1

34.   8
       9
       1

35.

x	0	1
0	6	6
1	8	8
2	6	6
3	6	6

36.   (a)   0 0 0 13 1 1 14 13 2 15 13 13 16 13 13   13

       (b)   0   10   11   12
              9   1   11   12
```
```

```
9    9    2   12
9    9    9    3
```

37.   (a)   1   (b)   1
2   2
3   3
4   4
5   5
6   6
7   7
8   8

38.   8

39.

f	0	1	2	3
0	8	7	8	7
1	7	7	8	7
2	7	7	8	7
3	7	7	7	7

40.   23

41.   The program will print an unpredictable value since array element **a[1][0]** has not been initialized. All arrays in C begin with a lower bound of 0. The **for** loop in this program begins with a **j** of 1 rather than 0.

42.

test	0	1	2
0	2	2	2
1	2	2	2
2	2	2	2
3	1	1	1

43.
```
#include <stdio.h>
#define SIZE 5
void main()
```

```
{
        int i, j, arr[SIZE][SIZE], sum = 0, diag_sum = 0, product = 1;

        for (i = 0; i < SIZE; i++)
                for (j = 0; j < SIZE; j++) {
                        scanf("%d", &arr[i][j]);
                        sum = sum + arr[i][j];
                }
        printf("sum = %d\n", sum);

        for (i = 0; i < SIZE; i++) {
                product = product * arr[i][2];
                diag_sum = diag_sum + arr[i][i];
        }
        printf("third column product = %d\n", product);
        printf("diagonal sum = %d\n", diag_sum);
}
```

44.   8
        11
        −2

45.   4   4   4   4   6   6   6   6   8   8   8   8
        2   4   4   4   4   4   6   6   6   6   6   8

46.   0   0
        6
        0   1
        12
        0   2
        24
        1   0
        48
        1   1
        96
        1   2
        192
        0   0
        0   1
        0   2
        ip! ip! array!
        1   0
        1   1
        1   2
        ip! ip! array!

47.

numbs	0	1	2	3
0	3	-1	-2	3
1	1	3	-2	4
2	2	3	3	5

48.   (a)

a	0	1	2	3
0	1	5	9	13
1	2	6	10	14
2	3	7	11	15
3	4	8	12	16

(b)   0 0 0 0 1 1 1 1 2 2 2 2 3 3 3 3

total = 36

49.

arr	0	1	2
0	-1	2	7
1	-2	9	5
2	-4	-3	-1
3	0	6	8

arr	0	1	2
0	15	16	17
1	-2	17	18
2	-4	-3	19
3	0	6	8

50.   printf("The number of males who are juniors is %d\n", st[1][0]);

51.   (a)   *function header*:   void swap(int *px, int *py)
                function prototype: void swap(int *, int *);

(b)   *function header*:   void sort(int a[], int n)
        function prototype: void sort(int [], int);

The function for Part (a) accepts two pointers to *scalars* (single memory locations). The function does not need to know that they point to elements of an array in the calling program. The function un Part (b), in contrasts, accepts a pointer (i.e., the array identifier itself) to the entire array for sorting.

52.   (a)   *Function **subsum** finds the sum of the **n**th row of array **x**, and* */*
                /* replaces each element in the **k**th column by that sum.* */*

```
void subsum(int x[][4], int n, int k)
{
        int i, sum = 0;

        for (i = 0; i < 4; i++)
                sum = sum + x[n][i];
        for (i = 0; i < 3; i++)
                x[i][k] = sum;
}
```

       (b)
```
int help[3][4];
void subsum(int [][4], int, int);
    ...
subsum(help, 2, 0);
```

53.   (a)   /* Function **print** prints the entire array.   */
```
void print(int x[][7])
{
        int i, j;

        for (i = 0; i < 13; i++) {
                for (j = 0; j < 7; j++)
                        printf("%5d", x[i][j]);
                printf("\n");
        }
}
```

       (b)   /* Function **prt** prints all array elements greater*/
                /* than 80 or less than 10.   */
```
void prt(int x[][7])
{
        int i, j;

        for (i = 0; i < 13; i++)
                for (j = 0; j < 7; j++)
                        if (x[i][j] > 80 || x[i][j] < 10)
                                printf("%5d", x[i][j]);
}
```

(c)   /* Function **printcoln** *prints the nth column*   */
        /* *of the array.*   */
        void printcoln(**int** x[][7], **int** n)
        {
                int i;

                if (n < 0 || n > 6) {
                        printf("ERROR: n is out of bounds.\n");
                        return;
                }

                for (i = 0; i < 7; i++)
                        printf("%d\n", x[i][n]);
        }

(d)   /* Function **printrev** *prints the array with the*   */
        /* *rows reversed.*   */
        void printrev(**int** x[][7])
        {
                int i, j;

                for (i = 12; i >= 0; i--) {
                        for (j = 0; j < 7; j++)
                                printf("%5d", x[i][j]);
                        printf("\n");
                }
        }

(e)   /* Function **largest** *returns the largest number* */
        /* *in the array.*   */
        int largest(**int** x[][7])
        {
                int i, j, largest;

                largest = x[0][0];
                for (i = 0; i < 13; i++)
                        for (j = 0; j < 7; j++)
                                if (x[i][j] > largest)
                                        largest = x[i][j];
                return largest;
        }

(f)   /* Function **largesubsc** *prints the subscript*   */
        /* *of the largest element of the array.*   */
        void largesubsc(**int** x[][7])

```
              {
                      int i, j, large;
                      int largest(int [][7]);

                      large = largest(x);
                      for (i = 0; i < 13; i++)
                              for (j = 0; j < 7; j++)
                                      if (x[i][j] == large) {
                                              printf("%d    %d\n", i, j);
                                              return;
                                      }
              }
```

54.
```
        #include <stdio.h>
        void main()
        {
                int x[100], i;
                float ave;
                FILE * datafile;
                float average(int [], int);
                void printstats(int [], int, float);

                datafile = fopen("datafile.dat", "r");
                i = 0;
                while (fscanf(datafile, "%d", &x[i]) != EOF)
                        i++;
                ave = average(x, i);
                printf("The average is %f\n", ave);
                printstats(x, i, ave);
                fclose(datafile);
        }

        float average(int x[], int n)
        {
                int i;
                float sum = 0.0;

                for (i = 0; i < n; i++)
                        sum = sum + x[i];
                return sum / n;
        }

        void printstats(int x[], int n, float average)
        {
                int i, even = 0, odd = 0, above = 0, below = 0;
```

```
                for (i = 0; i < n; i++) {
                        if (x[i] % 2 == 0)
                                even++;
                        else
                                odd++;
                        if (x[i] >= average)
                                above++;
                        else
                                below++;
                }
                printf("There were %d even numbers\n", even);
                printf("There were %d odd numbers\n", odd);
                printf("%d numbers were above the average\n", above);
                printf("%d numbers were below the average\n", below);
        }
```

55.
```
        int largest(int x[], int n)
        {
                int i, large;

                large = x[0];
                for (i = 1; i < n; i++)
                        if (x[i] > large)
                                large = x[i];
                return large;
        }
```

56.
```
        #include <string.h>
        #define TRUE 1
        #define FALSE 0
        void sortprint(char *name[], int age[], int n)
        {
                int hold, j, pass, switched = TRUE;
                char temp[20];

                for (pass = 0; pass < n-1 && switched == TRUE; pass++) {
                        switched = FALSE;
                        for (j = 0; j < n - pass - 1; j++)
                                if (age[j] < age[j + 1]) {
                                        switched = TRUE;
                                        hold = age[j];
                                        age[j] = age[j + 1];
                                        age[j + 1] = hold;
                                        strcpy(temp, name[j]);
```

```
                                        strcpy(name[j], name[j+1]);
                                        strcpy(name[j + 1], temp);
                        }
                }
        for (j = 0; j < n; j++)
                printf("%s     %d\n", name[j], age[j]);
}
```

function prototype: **void** sortprint(**char** * [], **int** [], **int**);

57.
```
#define SIZE 100
void func(int x[], int n)
{
        int temp[SIZE], counter[SIZE], i;

        /* copy array x into temporary array temp        */
        /* and initialize counter to zero.               */
        for (i = 0; i < n ; i++) {
                temp[i] = x[i];
                counter[i] = 1;
        }

        /* sort array temp.                              */
        sort(temp, n);

        /* count each item in array temp.                */
        for (i = 1; i < n; i++)
                if (temp[i] == temp[i - 1])
                        counter[i] = counter[i - 1] + 1;
        for (i = 0; i < n; i++)
                if (temp[i] != temp[i + 1])
                        printf("%d appeared %d times\n",
                                temp[i], counter[i]);

}
```

58.
```
#include <stdio.h>
#define SOLD 1
#define UNSOLD 0
void main()
{
        int theater[30][27], row, seat;

        for (row = 0; row < 30; row++)
                for (seat = 0; seat < 27; seat++)
```

```
                        theater[row][seat] = UNSOLD;

        printf("Enter the row and seat number of sold tickets: ");
        while (scanf("%d%d", &row, &seat) == 2) {
                theater[row][seat - 100] = SOLD;
                printf("Enter the row and seat number of sold tickets: ");
        }

        printf("Unsold Seats\n");
        for (row = 0; row < 30; row++)
                for (seat = 0; seat < 27; seat++)
                        if (theater[row][seat] == UNSOLD)
                                printf("row %d seat %d", row, seat + 100);
}
```

CHAPTER 10 - SORTING AND SEARCHING

1. (a) 5
    (b) 4

2.
```c
#define TRUE 1
#define FALSE 0
void sort(int x[], int n)
{
        int hold, j, pass, switched = TRUE;

        for (pass = 0; pass < n - 1 && switched == TRUE; pass++) {
                switched = FALSE;
                for (j = 0; j < n - pass - 1; j++)
                        if (x[j] > x[j + 1]) {
                                switched = TRUE;
                                hold = x[j];
                                x[j] = x[j + 1];
                                x[j + 1] = hold;
                        }
        }
}
```

3.
```c
#include <stdio.h>
#include <string.h>
#define SIZE 50
#define TRUE 1
#define FALSE 0
void main()
{
        int i, n, id[SIZE];
        float amount[SIZE];
        char name[SIZE][20];
        void bubblesort(char [][20], int [], float [], int);
        FILE * datafile;

        datafile = fopen("data.dat", "r");
        i = 0;
        while (fscanf(datafile, "%s%d%f",
                                name[i], &id[i], &amount[i]) != EOF)
                i++;
        fclose(datafile);
        n = i;
```

```
                bubblesort(name, id, amount, n);

                printf("CUSTOMER          ID      AMOUNT\n");
                for (i = 0; i < n; i++)
                        printf("%-20s%5d%10.2f\n", name[i], id[i], amount[i]);
        }

        void bubblesort(char name[][20], int id[], float amount[], int n)
        {
                int hold1, j, pass, switched = TRUE;
                float hold2;
                char hold3[20];

                for (pass = 0; pass < n - 1 && switched == TRUE; pass++) {
                        switched = FALSE;
                        for (j = 0; j < n - pass - 1; j++)
                                if (strcmp(name[j], name[j + 1]) > 0) {
                                        switched = TRUE;
                                        strcpy(hold3, name[j]);
                                        strcpy(name[j], name[j + 1]);
                                        strcpy(name[j + 1], hold3);
                                        hold1 = id[j];
                                        id[j] = id[j + 1];
                                        id[j + 1] = hold1;
                                        hold2 = amount[j];
                                        amount[j] = amount[j + 1];
                                        amount[j + 1] = hold2;
                                }
                }
        }
```

4.
```
        #include <stdio.h>
        #include <string.h>
        #define MAXSTUDENTS 25
        #define TRUE 1
        #define FALSE 0
        void main()
        {
                int i, j, n, exam[MAXSTUDENTS][10], tempexam[MAXSTUDENTS];
                char name[MAXSTUDENTS][10], tempname[MAXSTUDENTS][10];
                void avg(int []);
                int count(int []);
                void sort(char [][10], int [], int);
                FILE * datafile;
```

```
                    /* Part (a)                          */
                    datafile = fopen("data.dat", "r");
                    fscanf(datafile, "%d", &n);
                    for (i = 0; i < n; i++) {
                            fscanf(datafile, "%s", name[i]);
                            printf("%s\n", name[i]);
                            for (j = 0; j < 10; j++) {
                                    fscanf(datafile, "%d", &exam[i][j]);
                                    printf("%d   ", exam[i][j]);
                            }
                            /* Part (b) and Part (c)          */
                            avg(exam[i]);
                            /* Part (d)                       */
                            printf("Number of grades between 80 and 89: %d\n\n",
                                    count(exam[i]));
                    }
                    /* Part (e)                           */
                    for (i = 0; i < n; i++) {
                            strcpy(tempname[i], name[i]);
                            tempexam[i] = exam[i][4];
                    }
                    sort(tempname, tempexam, n);
                    /* Part (f)                           */
                    printf("\n\nName      Fifth Exam\n");
                    for (j = 0; j < n; j++)
                            printf("%-10s%10d\n", tempname[j], tempexam[j]);

                    printf("\nSecond lowest on fifth exam was %s\n", tempname[1]);
                    printf("Second highest on fifth exam was %s\n", tempname[n-2]);

            }

            void avg(int exam[10])
            {
                    int i;
                    float sum, average1, average2;

                    sum = 0;
                    for (i = 0; i < 5; i++)
                            sum = sum + exam[i];
                    average1 = sum / 5.0;
                    sum = 0;
                    for (i = 5; i < 10; i++)
                            sum = sum + exam[i];
                    average2 = sum / 5.0;
```

```
                printf("\n%5.1f  %5.1f\n", average1, average2);
                if (average1 == average2)
                        printf("Average of 1st five is the same as 2nd five.\n");
                else if (average1 > average2)
                        printf("Average of 1st five is greater than 2nd five.\n");
                else
                        printf("Average of 1st five is less than 2nd five\n");
        }

        int count(int exam[])
        {
                int i, cnt = 0;

                for (i = 0; i < 10; i++)
                        if (exam[i] >= 80 && exam[i] <= 89)
                                cnt++;
                return cnt;
        }

        /* Sort the arrays using a bubblesort              */
        void sort(char name[][10], int exam[], int n)
        {
                int hold1, j, pass, switched = TRUE;
                char hold2[10];

                for (pass = 0; pass < n - 1 && switched == TRUE; pass++) {
                        switched = FALSE;
                        for (j = 0; j < n - pass - 1; j++)
                                if (exam[j] > exam[j + 1]) {
                                        switched = TRUE;
                                        hold1 = exam[j];
                                        exam[j] = exam[j + 1];
                                        exam[j + 1] = hold1;
                                        strcpy(hold2, name[j]);
                                        strcpy(name[j], name[j + 1]);
                                        strcpy(name[j + 1], hold2);
                                }
                }
        }

5.      char name[10][20], temp[10];
        int i, pass, cand, n;

        for (pass = 0; pass < n - 1; pass++)
```

```
            for (cand = pass + 1; cand < n; cand++)
                    if (strcmp(name[pass], name[cand]) > 0) {
                            strcpy(temp, name[pass]);
                            strcpy(name[pass], name[cand]);
                            strcpy(name[cand], temp);
                    }
            for (i = 0; i < n; i++)
                    printf("%s\n", name[i]);
```

6.   In the linear search each element of the array is compared with the element being searched
      for. As soon as a match is found, there is no reason to continue searching through the
      remainder of the array. When a match is found, the integer variable **found** is set to *true*
      and the **while** loop is terminated.

7.
```
            for (pos = 0; pos < n; pos++)
                    if (item[pos] == key)
                            return pos;
            return -1;
```

8.   Binary searching of a sorted array is more efficient than linear searching of the same array.
      The more elements in the array, the greater the saving of the binary search. Moreover, if
      the element sought is not present, the binary search is even more efficient. A binary search
      takes only n comparisons, where 2^n is equal to the number of elements in the array. The
      linear search of 2^2 elements, will on the average require 2^{n-1} comparisons if the item is
      present, and 2^n comparisons if it is not. The bigger the value of n, the more advantageous
      is the binary search. For example, if $n = 1024$ the binary search will take 10 comparisons
      if the element is not present, whereas a linear search would take 1024 comparisons.

      The binary search requires the array to have been sorted beforehand; the linear search
      does not. Since sorting is expensive in time, if only a few searches are required and the
      array is not yet sorted, it pays to do the extra work of a linear search and not bother to
      sort. However, if many searches are to be done on the array, it is more efficient overall to
      sort the array first and then use the binary search.

9.
```
            char * linearsearch(int x[], int n, int key)
            {
                    int i;

                    for (i = 0; i < n; i++)
                            if (key == x[i])
                                    return "yes";
                    return "no";
            }
```

10.   linear   binary

(a)	8	3
(b)	10	4
(c)	2	2
(d)	9	4

CHAPTER 11 - STRING MANIPULATION IN C

1.   A string in C is declared as an array of characters. Since an array identifier is actually a pointer to the storage reserved for the array, it is often useful to consider a string identifier as a pointer to a character. All C string functions in the standard *string.h* library as well as the **%s** control character when used in the **printf** function assume that the string is terminated by the null character '\0'.

    For example, the declaration

            char line[20] = "Are You My Mother?"

results in the identifier **line** pointing to the character A in the following (in which each box represents a byte of memory):

A	r	e		Y	o	u		M	y		M	o	t	h	e	r	?	\0	

2.   `Horton Hears a  Who`

3.   The Cat
        In the Hat Comes Back!

4.   Each **%s** in the **scanf** function reads a series of characters and places them at the address pointed to by the associated identifier. It stops upon encountering a *white space* (e.g. blanks, tabs, and carriage returns) and automatically terminates the string with a \0. Thus it is an easy way of reading individual words from the input stream. However, since each **%s** terminates upon encountering a white space, it is unable to read more than one word at a time for each identifier. The **fgetc** function, on the other hand, reads a single character at a time from the input stream. Using the method of Exercise 3 and the **fgetc** function, the programmer may assemble a string consisting of several words. Note that unlike the **scanf** function, when using the **fgetc** function, a \0 must be explicitly placed at the end of the assembled string.

5.   `Duck, Donald is 35.0 years old`
        `Mouse, Mickey is 42.5 years old`
        `Boop, Betty is 28.2 years old`

        `The average age is 35.2`

6.   **scanf** expects the *address* of the identifier at which it is to store the value read. Thus the address operator (&) is applied to the variables **id** and **age** in order to return the address

of these variables to the **scanf** function. However, since **first** and **last** represent strings, and strings are implemented as arrays (See Exercise 1.), **first** and **last** are actually addresses (or pointers). The address operator is therefore not used.

7.
```
/* getline() allocates storage for and returns a */
/* pointer to a string read from stdin.          */
char * getline()
{
        int c, i;
        static char line[81];

        i = 0;
        while ((c = getchar()) != EOF && c != '\n' && i < 80) {
                line[i] = c;
                i++;
        }
        line[i] = '\0';
        return line;
}
```

8.
```
/* strlen(s) returns the length of s. This version*/
/* uses array notation.                            */
int strlen(char s[])
{
        int i;

        i = 0;
        while (s[i] != '\0')
                i++;
        return i;

}
```

```
/* strlen(s) returns the length of s. This version*/
/* uses pointer notation.                          */
int strlen(char *s)
{
        int i;

        for (i = 0; *s != 0; s++)
                i++;
        return i;
}
```

9.
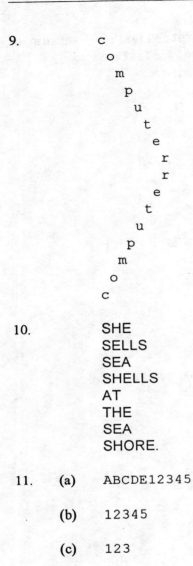

10.   SHE
        SELLS
        SEA
        SHELLS
        AT
        THE
        SEA
        SHORE.

11.   (a)   ABCDE12345

      (b)   12345

      (c)   123

      (d)   12345

      (e)   DE123

12.   Although an error message may not necessarily be produced, Statement (a) is in error. It
      is the programmer's responsibility to ensure that the target string is large enough to
      contain the target string concatenated with the source string *including* the \0 character.

      Statement (d) is in error for the same reason and may cause a system crash. **p + 5** points
      to the 5th character in **str2. strcpy** copies characters from its second argument to its first
      argument until a \0 is encountered thus overrunning the storage allocated for **str1**.

13.   Blanks at the end do count.

```
A blank is not a null string
The blank within quotes is
A legal character
5
6
A blank and a null string are different
bA blank and a null string are different
```

14.
```c
void reverse(char *string)
{
        int i, j;
        char c;

        j = strlen(string) - 1;
        for (i = 0; i < j; i++) {
                c = string[i];
                string[i] = string[j];
                string[j] = c;
                j--;
        }
}
```

15.   (a)
```c
int code;
   ...
printf("%d", (code % 100) / 10);
```

      (b)
```c
char word[5];
   ...
printf("%c", word[strlen(word)-2]);
```

16.   (a)   ABCBA
      (b)   (null)
      (c)   AA
      (d)   BA
      (e)   (null)
      (f)   bABC
      (g)   ABC123123
      (h)   (null)

17   7   15
            Monticello   LibertyNY   Fallsburg
            bigger
            LibeHuyNY
```
```

18.

Function	Returned value	Number of parameters	Type of each parameter
strcat	char *	2	char *, char *
strcmp	int	2	char *, char *
strcpy	char *	2	char *, char *
strlen	unsigned int	1	char *
strstr	char *	2	char *, char *

19.
```
TUVWXYZ    LMNOP        LMNOPTUVWXYZ
52
TU
XW
TU
XW□Q
```

In which □ represents an unprintable character resulting from attempting to print a \0.

20.
```
b    1
abA    3
aabAA    5
aaabAAA    7
aaaabAAAA    9
aaaaabAAAAA    11
aaaaaabAAAAAA    13
aaaaaaabAAAAAAA    15
aaaaaaaabAAAAAAAA    17
aaabAAA
AzAAA
```

CHAPTER 12 - STRUCTURES

1. (a) 14
    (b) 22
    (c) none - **student** is a *tag* name; no variables have been declared.
    (d) 1100

2. A *tag name serves* as a symbolic name for the structure definition; it does not allocate storage nor does it identify a memory location. A *structure variable*, on the other hand represents a location in memory which has been reserved for that variable. In Exercise 3(d), **student** is a *tag name*, and **st** is the name of a variable representing an array of structures.

3.   367.50

4.   printf("%d %d %s\n", breakfast.liquid, lunch.liquid, supper.solid);

5.   **struct** {
                char title[20], author[20], publisher[20];
                int catalog_no, year, pages;
                float price;
        } book;

6.   **struct** date {
                char month[3];
                int day, year;
        }

        struct name {
                char last[10], first[10], mi;
        }

        struct {
                struct name;
                struct date birthdate;
                float gpa;
                int id;
                struct date graduation;
                char major[10];
        } student;

7.   struct {
                float price;

```
                        int year, cylinders, horsepower;
                        char model[10], color[10];
                } ford, chevrolet, toyota;
```

8.   (a)   ```
             struct pupil{
                     char first[15], last[15];
                     int class_no, exams[5];
                     float average;
                     char grade;
             } student;
             ```

      (b)    ```
             scanf("%s%d", student.first, &student.class_no);
             ```

      (c)   ```
             void avg(struct pupil *pstudent)
             {
                     int sum = 0;

                     for (i = 0; i < 5; i++)
                             sum = sum + pstudent->exams[i];
                     pstudent->average = sum / 5.0;
             }
             ```

      (d)    ```
             void letter_grade(struct pupil *pstudent)
             {
                     if (pstudent->average >= 90)
                             pstudent->grade = 'A';
                     else if (pstudent->average >= 80)
                             pstudent->grade = 'B';
                     else if (pstudent->average >= 70)
                             pstudent->grade = 'C';
                     else if (pstudent->average >= 80)
                             pstudent->grade = 'D';
                     else
                             pstudent->grade = 'F';
             }
             ```

      (e)   ```
             void message(struct pupil student)
             {
                     if (student.class_no >= 600 && student.grade == 'F')
                             printf("%s %s\n", student.first, student.last);
                     else
                             printf("NO GOOD\n");
             }
             ```

9.    Sarah    137.50    NY
             ```

```
Mary    332.50   FL
Bill    160.00   CA
Total salary paid was 630.00
```

10. (a) printf("%s", division[0].regiment[3].company[9].captain);

    (b) division[5].regiment[2] = division[2].regiment[4];

    (c) **for** (i = 0; i < 10; i++)
            printf("%s\n", division[i].general);

11. printf("%s %s\n", father.haircolor, sibling[2].birthday);

12. (a) dtr = 0;
        for (i = 0; i < no_of_children; i++)
            if (strcmp(family[1].child[i].gender, "female") == 0 && dtr <= 3) {
                printf("%s %c %s\n",
                    family[1].child[i].name.first,
                    family[1].child[i].name.mi,
                    family[1].child[i].name.last);
                dtr++;
            }

    (b) sort(family[6].child, no_of_children);
        for (i = 0; i < no_of_children; i++)
            printf("%s %c %s\n",
                family[6].child[i].name.first,
                family[6].child[i].name.mi,
                family[6].child[i].name.last);

        void sort(**struct** kid child, **int** n)
        {
            int j, pass, switched = TRUE;
            struct kid temp;

            for (pass = 0; pass < n - 1 && switched == TRUE; pass++) {
                switched = FALSE;
                for (j = 0; j < n - pass - 1; j++)
                    if (strcmp(child[j].name.first, child[j + 1].name.first
                                                            > 0) {
                        switched = TRUE;
                        temp = child[j];
                        child[j] = child[j + 1];
                        child[j + 1] = temp;
                    }
        }
```
```

```
                        }
                }

(c)     n = 0;
        for (i = 0; i < 10; i++)
                if (strcmp(family[i].mother.maiden, family[i]. father.last) == 0)
                        n++;
        printf("%d %s %s\n",
                n,
                "wives have the same maiden names ",
                "as their husband's last name");

(d)     for (i = 0; i < 10; i++)
                if (strcmp(family[i].address.zip, "11210") == 0)
                        printf("%s %c %s\n%s\n%s, %s %s\n",
                                family[i].father.first,
                                family[i].father.mi,
                                family[i].father.last,
                                family[i].address.street,
                                family[i].address.city,
                                family[i].address.state,
                                family[i].address.zip);

(e)     printf("%s", family[2].child[1].name.first);

(f)     family[1].child[2].name.first

13.     #include <stdio.h>
        #include <string.h>
        #define TRUE 1
        #define FALSE 0
        #define MAXSTUDENTS 20

        struct student {
                char last[20], first[20], mi[2];
                char street[25], city[10], state[3], zip[6];
                int code[6], credits[6];
        };

        void main()
        {
                struct student st[MAXSTUDENTS];
                void sort(struct student[], int);

                int i, j, count;
```

```
                    FILE * datafile;

                    datafile = fopen("data.dat", "r");
                    i = 0;
                    while (fscanf(datafile, "%s%s%s%s%s%s%s",
                                st[i].first, st[i].mi, st[i].last,
                                st[i].street, st[i].city, st[i].state, st[i].zip) != EOF) {
                        for (j = 0; j < 6; j++)
                                fscanf(datafile, "%d%d", &st[i].code[j], &st[i].credits[j]);
                        i++;
                    }
                    fclose(datafile);
                    count = i;
                    sort(st, count);
                    for (i = 0; i < count; i++) {
                        printf("\n\n%s %s. %s\n%s\n%s, %s %s\n",
                                st[i].first, st[i].mi, st[i].last,
                                st[i].street, st[i].city, st[i].state, st[i].zip);
                        for (j = 0; j < 6; j++)
                                printf("%d  %d  ", st[i].code[j], st[i].credits[j]);
                    }
            }


            void sort(struct student st[], int n)
            {
                    int j, pass, switched = TRUE;
                    struct student temp;

                    for (pass = 0; pass < n - 1 && switched == TRUE; pass++) {
                        switched = FALSE;
                        for (j = 0; j < n - pass - 1; j++)
                                if (strcmp(st[j].zip, st[j + 1].zip) > 0) {
                                        switched = TRUE;
                                        temp = st[j];
                                        st[j] = st[j + 1];
                                        st[j + 1] = temp;
                                }
                    }
            }

14.         for (i = 0; i < 100; i++)
                    if (strcmp(empl[i].address.zip, "11210") == 0)
                        printf("%s %s %s\n%s\n%s, %s %s\n\n",
                                empl[i].name.first, empl[i].name.mi, empl[i].name.last,
```

```
                              empl[i].address.street, empl[i].address.city,
                    empl[i].address.state, empl[i].address.zip);


15.    (a)    for (i = 0; i < 35; i++)
                    printf("%s %s\n", section2[i].name.first, section2[i].name.last);


       (b)    sum = 0;
              for (i = 0; i < 35; i++)
                    sum = sum + section1[i].grade.midterm;
              average = sum / 35.0;


       (c)    void highest(struct section section1[], struct section section2[])
              {
                    int hifinal, i;
                    struct person hiname;

                    hifinal = section1[0].grade.final;
                    hiname = section1[0].name;
                    for (i = 0; i < 35; i++){
                          if (section1[i].grade.final > hifinal) {
                                hifinal = section1[i].grade.final;
                                hiname = section1[i].name;
                          }
                          if (section2[i].grade.final > hifinal) {
                                hifinal = section2[i].grade.final;
                                hiname = section2[i].name;
                          }
                    }
                    printf("Highest grade: %d by %s %s\n",
                          hifinal, hiname.first, hiname.last);
              }


       (d)    void best1(struct section section1[], struct section section2[])
              {
                    struct person hiname;

                    if (section1[0].grade.midterm > section2[0].grade.midterm &&
                       section1[0].grade.final > section2[0].grade.final)
                          printf("%s %s scored better on both exams\n",
                                section1[0].name.first, section2[0].name.last);
                    else  if (section1[0].grade.midterm < section2[0].grade.midterm
                             &&  section1[0].grade.final < section2[0].grade.final)
                          printf("%s %s scored better on both exams\n",
                                section1[0].name.first, section1[0].name.last);
                    else  if (section1[0].grade.midterm == section2[0].grade.midterm
```

```
                        && section1[0].grade.final == section2[0].grade.final)
                        printf("Both scored the same on both exams\n");
        }

16.   (a)   printf("%s %d %4.2f\n",
                        student[24].name.first,
                        student[24].credits.total,
                        student[24].gpa.overall);

      (b)   scanf("%s%s%f%f", student[0].name.first, student[0].name.last,
                        &student[0].gpa.last_term, &student[0].gpa.present_term);
            scanf("%s%s%f%f", student[49].name.first, student[49].name.last,
                        &student[49].gpa.last_term, &student[49].gpa.present_term);

      (c)   for (i = 0; i < MAXSTUDENTS; i++) {
                        student[i].credits.last_term = student[i].credits.present_term;
                        student[i].gpa.last_term = student[i].gpa.present_term;
            }

17.   (a)   110

      (b)   employee[5].rate = 25.50;

      (c)   for (i = 0; i < 10; i++) {
                        total = 0;
                        for (j = 0; j < 7; j++)
                                total = total + employee[i].hours_worked[j];
                        employee[i].pay = employee[i].rate * total;
            }

18.   (a)   long = aviscar[0].miles.ending - aviscar[0].miles.starting;
            for (i = 1; i < 10; i++) {
                        distance =  aviscar[i].miles.ending - aviscar[i].miles.starting;
                        if (distance > long) {
                                long = distance;
                                j = i;
                        }
            }
            printf("%s %f %f %f\n",
                        aviscar[j].modelname,
                        aviscar[j].rate;
                        aviscar[j].miles.starting, aviscar[j].miles.ending);

      (b)   sum1 = sum2 = 0;
            for (i = 0; i , 10; i++) {
```

```
            sum1 = sum1 + hertzcar[i].rate;
            sum2 = sum2 + aviscar[i].rate;
        }
        printf("Average HERTZ rate is %f", sum1 / 10.0);
        printf("Average AVIS rate is %f", sum2 / 10.0);
```

(c)   ```
        for (i = 0; i < 10; i++)
            if (hertzcar[i].daysout > 7)
                printf("%s\n", hertzcar[i].modelname);
        ```

(d)     ```
        for (i = 0; i < 10; i++)
            if (aviscar[i].rate > 15.37)
                printf("%s\n", aviscar[i].modelname);
        ```

(e)   ```
        for (i = 0; i < 10; i++) {
            if (strcmp(hertzcar[i].modelname, "CHRYSLER") == 0)
                printf("%d\n", hertzcar[i].daysout);
            if (strcmp(aviscar[i].modelname, "CHRYSLER") == 0)
                printf("%d\n", aviscar[i].daysout);
        }
        ```

19.  (a)     ```
        store[24].coffee_sold.quantity = store[0].coffee_sold.quantity +
                                         store[49].coffee_sold.quantity;
        ```

(b) (i)   `printf("%s\n", store[2].manager);`
     (ii)   `printf("%.2f\n", store[0].cake_sold.price);`
     (iii) `printf("%.2f\n", store[9].cake_sold.price);`
     (iv)   `printf("%.2f\n", store[10].coffee_sold.price);`
     (v)   ```
        for (i = 0; i < 50; i++) {
            total = 0;
            total = total + store[i].coffee_sold.quantity *
                            store[i].coffee_sold.price;
            total = total + store[i].cake_sold.quantity *
                            store[i].cake_sold.price;
            printf("Total receipts for store %d are %.2f\n", i, total);
        }
        ```

20.  (a)     *function invocation*:   `func(division);`
             *function prototype*:    **void** func(**struct** army []);
             *function header*:       **void** func(**struct** army division[])

     (b)     *function invocation*:   `func(division[9]);`
             *function prototype*:    void func(struct army);
             *function header*:       void func(struct army division);
        ```

(c)   As defined in Exercise 10, it is not possible to send to the function the information for a single regiment, because we have not specified a *tag name* for the structure of the regiment. We could, of course, send the information for the entire **division[6]** (as in Part (b)) and only refer to the individual regiment.

21.   (a)   *function invocation*:   func(family);
              function prototype: **void** func(**struct** relations []);
              function header: **void** func(**struct** relations family[])

       (b)   *function invocation*:   func(family[9]);
              function prototype: **void** func(**struct** relations);
              function header: **void** func(**struct** relations family)

22.   (a)   *function invocation*:   func(section1, section2);
              function prototype: **void** func(**struct** section [], **struct** section[]);
              function header: **void** func(**struct** section s1[], **struct** section s2[])

23.   *function invocation*:   print_and_count(family);

```
void print_and_count(struct relations family[])
{
        int i, j, count;

        for (i = 0; i < 10; i++) {
                count = 0;
                for (j = 0; j < 5; j++)
                        if (strcmp(family[i].child[j].name.last,
                                        family[i].father.last) != 0)
                                count++;
                printf("%d %s %d %s\n",
                        count,
                        "children in family",
                        i,
                        "have different last names from their father's");
        }
}
```

24.   (a)   printf("%d %s\n", library[43].bookcode, library[43].authorname);

       (b)   **for** (i = 0; i < 3; i++)
                      printf("%s\n", library[6].subject[i]);
              for (i = 0; i < 3; i++)
                      printf("%s\n", library[7].subject[i]);

       (c)   **int** pagecount(**struct** book library[])

```
                    {
                            int i, count = 0;

                            for (i = 0; i < 100; i++)
                                    if (library[i].pages >= 250)
                                            count++;
                            if (count == 0)
                                    printf("NONE")
                            return count;
                    }
```

25.   (a)
```
       struct pupil {
               char last[15], first[15];
               int class-no;
               int exam[5];
               float average;
               char grade;
       } student[25];
```

(b)
```
       i = 0;
       while (scanf("%s%d", student[i].last, &student[i].class_no) != EOF)
               i++;
```

(c)
```
       void compute_avg(struct pupil student[])
       {
               int i, j, sum;

               for (i = 0; i < 25; i++) {
                       sum = 0;
                       for (j = 0; j < 5; j++)
                               sum = sum + student[i].exam[j];
                       student[i].average = sum / 5.0;
               }
       }
```

(d)
```
       void assign_grade(struct pupil student[])
       {
               int i;

               for (i = 0; i < 25; i++)
                       if (student[i].average >= 90)
                               student[i].grade = 'A';
                       else if (student[i].average >= 80)
                               student[i].grade = 'B';
                       else if (student[i].average >= 70)
```

```
                                     student[i].grade = 'C';
                         else if (student[i].average >= 60)
                                     student[i].grade = 'D';
                         else
                                     student[i].grade = 'F';
        }
```

(e)   **void** print_msg(**struct** pupil student[])
```
        {
                int i;

                for (i = 0; i < 25; i++)
                        if (student[i].class_no >= 600 && student[i].grade == 'F')
                                printf("%s %s\n", student[i].first, student[i].last);
        }
```

26.   (a)   **struct** info {
```
                        char first[10], last[15], ssno[9];
                        float gpa;
                        int currno, grades[5];
                } student;
```

(b)   **void** printinfo(**struct** info * pstudent)
```
        {
                int i;

                printf("Student name: %s %s\n", pstudent->first, pstudent->last);
                printf("Social security number: %s\n", pstudent->ssno);
                printf("GPA: %4.2f\n", pstudent->gpa);
                printf("Curriculum number: %d\n", pstudent->currno);
                for (i = 0; i < 5; i++)
                        printf("Test %d: %d\n", i, pstudent->grades[i]);
        }
```

(c)   **struct** info students[30];

(b)   **void** printinfo2(**struct** info * pstudent[ ], int n)
```
        {
                int i, j;

                for (j = 0; j < n; j++) {
                        printf("\n\nStudent #%d\n", j);
                        printf("Student name: %s %s\n",
                                        pstudent[j]->first, pstudent[j]->last);
                        printf("Social security number: %s\n", pstudent[j]->ssno);
```

```
                     printf("GPA: %4.2f\n", pstudent[j]->gpa);
                     printf("Curriculum number: %d\n", pstudent[j]->currno);
                     for (i = 0; i < 5; i++)
                             printf("Test %d: %d\n", i, pstudent[j]->grades[i]);
             }
     }
```

27.
```
    /* structure declaration */
    struct employee {
            char first[10], last[10];
            float rate, hours;
    };

    /* Function returns the pay of a single employee. */
    float computepay(struct employee worker)
    {
            return worker.rate * worker.hours;
    }
```

28.
```
    /* Function returns both the average and corresponding grade. */
    void computegrade(struct student *p_student)
    {
            float sum = 0.0, hwavg;
            int i;

            for (i = 0; i < 5; i++)
                    sum = sum + p_student->homework[i];
            hwavg = sum / 5;

            p_student->average = 0.3 * p_student->midterm +
                                 0.3 * p_student->final +
                                 0.4 * hwavg;

            if (p_student->average >= 90)
                    p_student->grade = 'A';
            else if (p_student->average >= 80)
                    p_student->grade = 'B';
            else if (p_student->average >= 70)
                    p_student->grade = 'C';
            else if (p_student->average >= 60)
                    p_student->grade = 'D';
            else
                    p_student->grade = 'F';
    }
```

```
29.        #include <stdio.h>
           #include <string.h>
           #define TRUE 1
           #define FALSE 0
           #define MAXNUMBER 20

           struct person {
                  char last[20], first[20];
           };

           /* Function sorts by last name. */
           void sort(struct person prsn[], int n)
           {
                  int j, pass, switched = TRUE;
                  struct person temp;

                  for (pass = 0; pass < n - 1 && switched == TRUE; pass++) {
                      switched = FALSE;
                      for (j = 0; j < n - pass - 1; j++)
                          if (strcmp(prsn[j].last, prsn[j + 1].last) > 0) {
                              switched = TRUE;
                              temp = prsn[j];
                              prsn[j] = prsn[j + 1];
                              prsn[j + 1] = temp;
                          }
                  }
           }

           void main()
           {
                  struct person name[MAXNUMBER];
                  void sort(struct person[], int);
                       ...

30.        #include <stdio.h>
           #include <string.h>
           #define MAXNUMBER 20

           struct person {
                  char last[20], first[20], phone[9];
           };

           /* Function returns the name corresponding to a given phone   */
           /* number or an error message if the phone number is not found.   */
           struct person search(struct person prsn[], char phonenum[], int n)
```

```
        {
                int i;
                struct person found;

                for (i = 0; i < n; i++)
                        if (strcmp(phonenum, prsn[i].phone) == 0)
                                return prsn[i];

                strcpy(found.first, "NOT");
                strcpy(found.last, "FOUND");
                strcpy(found.phone, phonenum);
                return found;
        }

        void main()
        {
                struct person item[MAXNUMBER], name_and_phone;
                /* Function prototype */
                struct person search(struct person[], char[], int);
                        ...

                /* Function invocation */
                name_and_phone = search(item, phonenum, count);
                        ...
```

31.
```
        #include <stdio.h>
        #include <string.h>
        #define TRUE 1
        #define FALSE 0
        #define MAXSTUDENTS 20

        struct student {
                char last[20], first[20], mi[2];
                int id;
                float grade;
        };

        /* Function sorts the student structure in grade order. */
        void sort(struct student st[], int n)
        {
                int j, pass, switched = TRUE;
                struct student temp;

                for (pass = 0; pass < n - 1 && switched == TRUE; pass++) {
                        switched = FALSE;
```

```
                for (j = 0; j < n - pass - 1; j++)
                    if (st[j].grade > st[j + 1].grade) {
                            switched = TRUE;
                            temp = st[j];
                            st[j] = st[j + 1];
                            st[j + 1] = temp;
                    }
        }
}

/* Function searches the student array by id.        */
struct student search(struct student item[], int id, int n)
{
        int i;
        struct student found;

        for (i = 0; i < n; i++)
                if (id == item[i].id)
                        return item[i];

        strcpy(found.first, "NOT");
        strcpy(found.last, "FOUND");
        found.id = id;
        return found;
}

void main()
{
        struct student st[MAXSTUDENTS], found;
        int count, id;

        /* Function prototypes */
        void sort(struct student[], int);
        struct student search(struct student [], int id, int n);
            ...

        /* Function invocations */
        sort(st, count);
            ...

        found = search(st, id, count);
            ...
```

CHAPTER 13 - NUMBER SYSTEMS

1.   (a) $10^2 = 100$ $10^1 = 10$ $10^0 = 1$

      (b) $123 = (1 \times 10^2) + (2 \times 10^1) + (3 \times 10^0)$
             $321 = (3 \times 10^2) + (2 \times 10^1) + (1 \times 10^0)$

2.
```
char ch;
int i;
 ...
i = (int) (ch - '0');
```

3.
```
char ch;
int i;
 ...
ch = (char) ('0' + i);
```

4.
```
int convert(char str[])
{
        return (str[0] - '0') * 100 + (str[1] - '0') * 10 + (str[2] - '0');
}
```

5.
```
char *dstring(int i)
{
        static char str[4];

        str[0] = (char) ('0' + i / 100);
        str[1] = (char) ('0' + (i % 100) / 10);
        str[2] = (char) ('0' + i % 10);
        str[3] = '\0';
        return str;
}
```

6.   0, 1, 10, 11, 100, 101, 110, 111, 1000, 1001, 1010

7.   0, 1, 2, 3, 4, 5, 6, 7, 8, 9, A, B, C, D, E, F, 10, 11, 12, 13, 14

8.   4   4

9. $111 = (1 \times 2^2) + (1 \times 2^1) + (1 \times 2^0)$

10.   (a) $0x111 = (1 \times 16^2) + (1 \times 16^1) + (1 \times 16^0)$
      (b) $0x9A0 = (9 \times 16^2) + (10 \times 16^1) + (0 \times 16^0)$

11. (a) 11001001
     (b) 100000000
     (c) 1011110
     (d) 1010
     (d) 1111101000

12. (a) 1000000001   (b) 1001010110
     (c) 10010100   (d) 10000
     (e) 1000000000000   (f) 110110101101
     (g) 1101110000010000   (h) 110000001011
     (i) 101010111100

13. (a) 1F4
     (b) 2C3
     (c) 12
     (d) 457
     (e) 4D0

14. (a) 13   (b) 4   (c) 10   (d) 5
     (e) 101   (f) 277   (g) 113   (h) 682
     (i) 36   (j) 102   (k) 65   (l) 508

15. (a) D   (b) 4   (c) A   (d) 5
     (e) 65   (f) 115   (g) 71   (h) 2AA
     (i) 24   (j) 66   (k) 41   (l) 1FC

16. A number which begins with a 0x is interpreted as a hexadecimal number, while a number which begins with a 0 is interpreted as an octal (base-8) number. Thus 10 = 10 (ten); 010 = 8; and 0x10 = 16.

17. (a) 0230_8
     (b) 1010000100_2
     (c) 213_{10}

18. (a) $1000010_2 = 66_{10}$
     (b) $1001000_2 = 72_{10}$
     (c) $100110010_2 = 306_{10}$
     (d) $1001110110_2 = 630_{10}$

FINAL EXAMINATION 1

Part 1

1.
```
??    20    30    40    50    60    70

3    0    20    40    41    50    60    170    80    1

-2    0    21    40    42    50    61    170    -2    1
```

2.
```
c is 5, d is 0
5 20 7 5
in change 24 100 4
24 100 5
in change 5 8 1005
5 8 6
```

3. (a)
```
6 -6
0 -13
-13 -20
outside -13 -20
```

   (b)
```
outside -1 3
```

   (c)
```
10 -3
7 -10
-3 -17
outside -3 -17
```

4.
```
HIJK ABCDE
ABCDEHIJK
case 1
54
AB
EQ
AB
EQ■f
```

5. (a)
```
beta
delta
```

   (b)
```
alpha
delta
```

(c)   ```
gamma
delta
```

6.    (a)    **void** changetoavg(**double** numbs[], **int** n)
```
{
        int i;
        double sum = 0.0, average;

        for (i = 0; i < n; i++)
                sum = sum + numbs[i];
        average = sum / n;
        print("%f\n", average);
        for (i = 0; i < n; i++)
                numbs[i] = average;
}
```

(b)    *function call*:        changetoavg(numbs, 20);
```
                        for (i = 0; i < 20; i++)
                                printf("%f ", numbs[i]);
```

*function prototype*:    **void** changetoavg(**double** [], **int**);

*declarations*:        **double** xyz[100];

7.    (a)    **struct** {
```
        char first[15], last[15];
        int cc_no;
        float exams[4], average;
        char grade;
} student;
```

(b)    scanf("%s%d", student.first, &student.cc_no);

(c)    student.average = (student.exam[0] + student.exam[1] + student.exam[2]
                        + student.exam[3]) / 4;

(d)    **if** (student.cc_no >= 600 & student.grade == 'F')
                printf("%s   %s", student.first, student.last);
    **else**
                printf("No good");
```

Part II Short answer questions

A.   (a)   74
       (b)   1110011
       (c)   12 bits - each hexadecimal digit requires 4 bits.
       (d)   10100
       (e)   (1)   111111
               (2)   0x3F

B.   (1)   c
       (2)   e
       (3)   c
       (4)   d
       (5)   b
       (6)   b
       (7)   e
       (8)   d
       (9)   a

Part III

```c
#include <stdio.h>
#include <string.h>
#define TRUE 1
#define FALSE 0

struct pupil {
        char first[20], last[20];
        float gpa;
};

void main()
{
        int i, n;
        struct pupil student[100];

        void sort(struct pupil [], int);
        float average(struct pupil [], int);

        scanf("%d", &n);
        for (i = 0; i < n; i++)
                scanf("%s%s%f", student[i].first, student[i].last,
                                                &student[i].gpa);

        sort(student, n);
        for (i = 0; i < n; i++)
```

```
                    printf("%10s%s, %s   %4.1f\n", " ",
                        student[i].last, student[i].first, student[i].gpa);
                printf("\n\n\nAverage = %4.1f\n", average(student, n));
}


void sort(struct pupil student[], int n)
{
        int j, pass, switched = TRUE;
        float temp;
        char hold[20];

        for (pass = 0; pass < n - 1 && switched == TRUE; pass++) {
                switched = FALSE;
                for (j = 0; j < n - pass; j++)
                        if (student[j].gpa < student[j+1].gpa) {
                                switched = TRUE;
                                temp = student[j].gpa;
                                student[j].gpa = student[j+1].gpa;
                                student[j+1].gpa = temp;
                                strcpy(hold, student[j].first);
                                strcpy(student[j].first, student[j+1].first);
                                strcpy(student[j+1].first, hold);
                                strcpy(hold, student[j].last);
                                strcpy(student[j].last, student[j+1].last);
                                strcpy(student[j+1].last, hold);
                        }
        }
}


float average(struct pupil student[], int n)
{
        int i;
        float sum = 0;

        for (i = 0; i < n; i++)
                sum = sum + student[i].gpa;
        return sum / n;
}
```

FINAL EXAMINATION 2

Part I

1.

100	100	100
101	200	1200
102	102	1102
103	35	-7
104	104	1040
105	104	-7
106	110	1110
107	107	107

2.
```
7 12

WashiYgton Adams GeorgieX
bigger
GeHrhieX
```

3.   (a)
```
In changes: -1 5 101
In main: -1 5 100
In changes: 95 1000 16
In main: 1000 15 95
```

(b)   i.   invalid - The first argument to the function is expected to be **a pointer** (e.g., the address of the variable **a**).

ii.   valid

4.   (a)
```
3    2
1    1
0    1
3   -1
-1    2
```

(b)   3   4   120
       9   4   220
      15   4   220

5.   (a)   **5 2 0**   i.e., the fifth line

      (b)   1   -7   5   bad
             1   2   3   indifferent
             5   5   5   good
             1   2   0   indifferent

6.
```c
#include <stdio.h>
void main()
{
        int grade;
        char letter;
        char curvedletgrade(int);

        scanf("%d", &grade);
        letter = curvedletgrade(grade);
        printf("%d   %c", grade, letter);
}

char curvedletgrade(int mark)
{
        if (mark >= 85)
                return 'A';
        else if (mark >= 70)
                return 'B';
        else if (mark >= 60)
                return 'C';
        else
                return 'D';
}
```

7.   (a)   `printf("%f   %s", library[34].code, library[34].authorname);`

      (b)
```c
for (i = 6; i <= 7; i++)
        for (j = 0; j < 3; j++)
                printf("%d   ", library[i].subject[j]);
```

      (c)
```c
count = 0;
for (i = 0; I < 100; i++)
        if (library[i].pages >= 250)
                count++;
```

```
        if (count > 0)
                printf"%d", count)
        else
                printf("NONE");
```

Part II Conversions and Multiple Choice

A. 1. 111000
    2. 0x3B
    3. 11111000
    4. 62
    5. 45
    6. Two bytes are equivalent to sixteen bits.

B. 1. b
    2. c
    3. e
    4. c
    5. d
    6. d

Part III

```
        #include <stdio.h>
        void main()
        {
                char sentence[81];
                int i;
                int countwords(char *);
                void changesentence(char *);

                i = 0;
                while ((sentence[i] = getchar()) != EOF) {
                        i++;
                        while ((sentence[i] = getchar()) != EOF && sentence[i] != '.')
                                i++;
                        if (sentence[i] == EOF)
                            break;
                        sentence[i+1] = '\0';
                        printf("%s\n", sentence);

                        printf("The number of words is %d.\n",
                                countwords(sentence));
```

```
                 changesentence(sentence);
                 printf("%s\n\n", sentence);

                 /* get the next sentence, if any. */
                 i = 0;
         }
         printf("THE END\n");
}
```

```
/* countwords counts the number of words in a sentence assuming    */
/* there is only one blank between each word and the last word     */
/* is followed by a period.                                        */
int countwords(char * sentence)
{
         int i, count = 1;

         i = 0;
         while (sentence[i] != '\0') {
                 if (sentence[i] == ' ')
                         count++;
                 i++;
         }
         return count;
}
```

```
/* changesentence encodes a sentence as specified in the assignment. */
void changesentence(char * sentence)
{
         int i;

         i = 0;
         while (sentence[i] != '\0') {
                 switch (sentence[i]) {
                         case 'A':    sentence[i] = 'V';    break;
                         case 'E':    sentence[i] = 'P';    break;
                         case 'I':    sentence[i] = '$';    break;
                         case 'O':    sentence[i] = 'F';    break;
                         case 'U':    sentence[i] = 'B';    break;
                         case ' ':    sentence[i] = 'J';    break;
                 }
                 i++;
         }
}
```